"JEAN FLEMING is one of the godliest women I know. She has lived the contents of this book and proven them as a means of God's transforming grace in her own life. Moreover, the Lord has greatly blessed the use of these spiritual lessons in her speaking and discipleship ministries with other women. I am confident that He will also bless this book and help many in the practical and heart issues of their pursuit of intimacy with God and a more disciplined daily Christian walk."

—DON WHITNEY,
assistant professor of spiritual formation,
Midwest Baptist Seminary, and author of
Spiritual Disciplines for the Christian Life

FEEDING YOUR SOUL

A Quiet Time Handbook

JEAN FLEMING

NAVPRESS ◐
BRINGING TRUTH TO LIFE
P.O. Box 35001, Colorado Springs, Colorado 80935

OUR GUARANTEE TO YOU

We believe so strongly in the message of our books that we are making this quality guarantee to you. If for any reason you are disappointed with the content of this book, return the title page to us with your name and address and we will refund to you the list price of the book. To help us serve you better, please briefly describe why you were disappointed. Mail your refund request to: NavPress, P.O. Box 35002, Colorado Springs, CO 80935.

The Navigators is an international Christian organization. Our mission is to reach, disciple, and equip people to know Christ and to make Him known through successive generations. We envision multitudes of diverse people in the United States and every other nation who have a passionate love for Christ, live a lifestyle of sharing Christ's love, and multiply spiritual laborers among those without Christ.

NavPress is the publishing ministry of The Navigators. NavPress publications help believers learn biblical truth and apply what they learn to their lives and ministries. Our mission is to stimulate spiritual formation among our readers.

ISBN 1-57683-144-2

Cover photo by SuperStock, Inc.

Some of the anecdotal illustrations in this book are true to life and are included with the permission of the persons involved. All other illustrations are composites of real situations, and any resemblance to people living or dead is coincidental.

Printed in the United States of America

Library of Congress Cataloging-in-Publication Data
Fleming, Jean.
    Feeding your soul : a quiet time handbook / Jean Fleming.
       p. cm.
    Includes bibliographical references.
    ISBN 1-57683-144-2 (pbk.)
    1. Devotion.   I. Title.
BV4815.F57   1999   99-23605
248.3—dc21   CIP

2 3 4 5 6 7 8 9 10 11 12 13 14 15 / 02 01 00

For my husband,
Roger Fleming,
whose heart for God has been an example,
an encouragement, and a refuge for me.

Contents

Introduction —
A Word to the Reader

Tom's spiritual life was flat. Although this military officer led Bible studies, the vitality had drained out of his own experience with God. When he made this complaint to my husband, Roger probed to uncover something that might help him. One of the first areas of inquiry was his devotional life. When Roger discovered that Tom had never cultivated the practice of spending regular time alone with the Lord, he launched him on a transforming journey. After receiving some practical tips, Tom began to rise earlier to meet with God. Almost immediately, coworkers inquired about the change in him, his wife made a deeper commitment to the Lord, and family members came to Christ. His experience went from flat to vibrant, and he says quiet time spent with God made the difference.

Perhaps, like Tom, your spiritual life has dried out. Or you may be an eager new believer — you want to know God and live for Him, but you've never heard of quiet time. Maybe you've tried quiet time before, but feel discouraged — or even defeated. You may be a person who has met with the Lord regularly for years, but the freshness is gone; you're in a deep rut and need a little stimulation to get out. Or maybe quiet times with God have been so meaningful to you that you'd like to help others begin the practice.

Whatever your situation, this book is designed to help you meet with God in a more meaningful way. The book is laid out *sequentially*.

It gets you started meeting with God on a daily basis and progresses through instruction that will keep you going over a lifetime.

Each chapter concludes with a brief *summary*, a "Making It Personal" section to help you apply the material, and *questions* for individual reflection or for use in a discussion group. Quiet time is an individual pursuit—one person meeting alone with God—but the support and stimulation of other believers is a powerful aid to consistency. Consider using the book privately in your time with God and then forming a small group for discussion and encouragement.

If you are just beginning quiet time, an incredible journey awaits you. If you have stumbled along in the past, take fresh heart. If you just need a little boost to get you over a rough place, I hope you will find it here.

May you find richer communion with Him.

"I WILL MEET WITH YOU"

Six times in the book of Exodus, God says, "I will meet with you." Five short words. The simplicity and economy of the statement belies the profound implication. God, Creator of all that is, will meet with you. God, ruler of universe upon universe, will meet with you. The Word made flesh will meet with you. God, Who died in your place and rose again, will meet with you. God, Who reigns in heaven, Lord of all, Who will come again, will meet with you.

This is an unthinkable phenomenon. Shocking. Staggering. Terrifying. Electrifying. Wonderful! God will meet with you? Who would have the nerve to propose such an idea? The proposal is all the more exhilarating because God Himself suggests the arrangement. God's desire for relationship with you seeps from the pores of those five words.

If we would accept God's invitation we must come God's way. His invitation is wonderfully gracious, but it includes His conditions as to who may come.

God met with Moses in a special place called the Holy of Holies (see Exodus 25:22), but after Moses died only the one designated as High Priest could enter this sacred place and only once

continued on next page

each year when he brought blood from a sacrificial animal. No other Israelite had such honor.

Then Jesus Christ opened the way for all to enter God's presence. When Jesus Christ died on the cross He became our eternal High Priest and He entered the true Holy of Holies in heaven with His own blood. The Old Testament picture is now fulfilled in our Lord Jesus Christ. God's way for us is that we come by faith in the blood sacrifice Jesus paid for us on the Cross. All who believe may come, and the Bible says we may come boldly at any time to find audience with the King of kings and Lord of lords.

Communion with God is deeply personal and this book contains a great variety of experiences and methods people have used to meet with God. The wonderfully open invitation to meet with our God must be married with a holy wonder that He allows such as we are to enter His presence. As we learn to approach Him let us remember the priceless sacrifice made by our Lord Jesus Christ to make this audience possible for us.

How does a mere man or woman—a person like you or me—respond to God's offer to meet with us? How will you reply to His invitation? Will you echo His words of friendship and say, "I will meet with You, Lord"?

Feb. 23, 1834—
Sabbath. Rose early to seek God, and
found him whom my soul loveth. Who
would not rise early to meet such company?

—FROM THE JOURNAL OF ROBERT MURRAY M'CHEYNE[1]

For I greet him the days I meet him,
and bless when I understand . . .
That guilt is hushed by, hearts are
flushed by and melt

—GERARD MANLEY HOPKINS[2]

ONE

Enjoying a Relationship with God

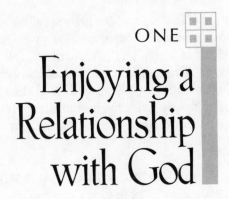

NEAR THE END OF MY SENIOR YEAR OF HIGH SCHOOL, SITTING WALL to wall with five hundred other students on the ballroom floor of the Flanders Hotel in Ocean City, New Jersey, I confronted a realm of possibility I had never considered: God wanted a relationship with me. The speaker moved carefully through ideas new to me: God loved me, wanted to be friends with me, and died on the cross—in my place—that it might be so.

I came to this youth rally at the ocean hoping that the breeze off the Atlantic might put fresh heart into me. I was seventeen and already disillusioned. Sin had nibbled some sizable holes inside me and I felt bruised. I was spiritually ignorant and knew little apart from what the speaker said, but the thought of being cleansed from my sins and beginning a friendship with God moved me. The meeting was barely over when I pushed through the crowd and made my way to my fourth-floor room to be alone, to pray. "Lord, I want what you did on the cross to count for me. I want to belong to You."

That brief prayer opened the door to my relationship with God. All relationships start with an initial meeting. But unless something more happens, it remains only an encounter, never developing into a relationship. Relationships must be cultivated. Friendships require time and communication. Every friendship takes effort.

The Bible teaches that our highest calling and greatest joy in life is friendship with God. Many years ago when the catechists defined the chief end of humankind, they wrote: "To glorify God and to enjoy Him forever." Throughout the ages, men and women who understood that a meaningful friendship with God doesn't just happen have reserved part of their day to give full attention to God. This practice has been called by many names; one of them is *quiet time*.

CULTIVATING A RELATIONSHIP WITH GOD

In the 1950s, a group of mature Christian men discussed the questions: "How do we help new believers develop a relationship with God? What are the most critical and basic elements that will help them grow in their new life with Christ?" They concluded that quiet time and memorizing Bible verses were the two most important practices to establish believers in the faith and keep them growing.

More recently one of the men was asked if, after all these years, he would still choose quiet time and Scripture memory as the most fundamental helps for becoming established in the faith.

His answer? "I'm more convinced than ever."

I, too, am convinced. I believe that quiet time is the single most important thing you can do to feed your soul.

You may ask, "What is quiet time, anyway?" or, "Why is it so important?" This book is designed to answer those questions and to help you explore and develop your relationship with God through the practice of quiet time.

WHAT DOES IT MEAN TO HAVE A RELATIONSHIP WITH GOD?

When you believed and embraced Jesus as your Savior and Lord, you became related to God in a literal sense (see Romans 8:15-16). The Bible speaks of God as your Father and Jesus as your brother. You are related by blood. Kin. But God intends for you to move beyond the birth certificate to a very personal and daily experience with Him. God wants you to live connected to Him all day long. He desires to use the circumstances you face every day as points of intimate contact with Him.

Say, for example, that you face financial stress. This situation in your life becomes a place of convergence with God. You allow financial pressure to link you to God. You seek God's help. You come to Him with an open, expectant heart. You read His Word and regard it as His personal communication to you. You trust Him for encouragement, wisdom, perseverance, and direction. In this way, the circumstances of your life come to serve you, to draw you into deeper experience with God. Quiet time will help you cultivate this growing relationship.

WHAT IS QUIET TIME, ANYWAY?

A few years ago, after I mentioned quiet time in a talk, a very animated lady told me how much she enjoyed her quiet times. She had quiet time most mornings and wished that she had begun the practice years before. As we talked, I inquired about how she used the time. She explained that she gets up early and has a cup of coffee while she writes letters. No question about it—it was *quiet* and it was *time*. But somewhere along the way, she missed the point.

When I say *quiet time*, I mean an appointment with God, a block of time chiseled out of your day and set apart for God, a time of private worship. Think of it as a date with God. A time for just the two of you. The term "quiet time" is not found in the Bible, but over the years this practice has been called by various names. Each sheds a bit more light on the subject.

What Does God Say About Quiet Time?

God does not command quiet time, but He does command devotion. In fact, Jesus called it the greatest commandment: "Love the Lord your God with all your heart and with all your soul and with all your strength" (Deuteronomy 6:5, Matthew 22:37).

Terms such as "devotions," "quiet time," and "appointment with God" don't appear in Scripture, but the idea of setting apart regular time with God does. The Bible repeatedly makes reference to Jesus, the Son of God, withdrawing to be alone with the Father (see Mark 1:35, Luke 5:16). Daniel set aside times each day to pray (see Daniel 6:10-11,13). David often mentions specific times set apart to meet with

God. Because these spiritual giants made dates with God an important part of their lives, we should explore the practice further.

TIME SET APART FOR GOD

Morning Watch. This name conjures up the image of a watchman at his post early in the morning. All is still. No one stirs. He is alone with his thoughts and his God. Watchful and alert, he waits for the sun to rise. Psalm 130:6 expresses this idea: "My soul waits for the Lord more than those on watch wait for the morning, more than those on watch wait for the morning."

Devotions. Very simply, the term "devotions" speaks of our desire to live a life devoted to God. To begin, we set aside a portion of each day as an act of devotion. We reserve this time as holy, set apart for one thing: meeting with God.

Appointment with God. Clearly, this indicates an arrangement to meet God at a particular time and place. It is a date, a rendezvous.

Quiet time. While this is the term I like best, it could be misleading. Although the ideal setting for a quiet time might be a hushed, serene spot, that isn't always possible. Quiet times are not always quiet. I've kept my date with God while my children were playing nearby; at other times, amid the buzz at a fast food restaurant or on an airplane at 35,000 feet. "Quiet" refers primarily to our heart's gaze rather than our physical setting. The idea is to silence our compulsive inner restlessness and come into God's presence. The "quiet" in quiet time doesn't require physical silence, but there is no way to get around the "time" part. We must make time for God.

Quiet time is about making space in your life every day to promote a deepening bond with Jesus Christ, a time of mingling Life to life. Quiet time is not a solitary exercise, nor an independent enterprise. It is a fellowship, an interchange, a communion, a friendship, a date with God.

Quiet time is about cultivating a relationship with God. It is, of course, possible for a person to have a relationship with God and *not* set aside alone time with Him every day. It is also possible for a person to religiously set aside time for Bible reading and prayer and not have a relationship with God.

Some people tell me they talk to God throughout the day and wonder if it is still necessary to set aside special time for fellowship with Him. I think it is. No relationship flourishes without some face-to-face time when we give our total attention to the other person. In our busy age, we pride ourselves on accomplishing multiple tasks at one time. We talk on the phone, read the newspaper, and watch the baseball game—all while helping our children with their homework. This may seem necessary, even admirable, but unless we give some undivided attention to our closest relationships, they will wither.

Brother Lawrence (1611–1691) was a monk who worked in a monastery kitchen and lived in continual communion with God all day, every day. He prayed as he scrubbed the pots and cleaned the kitchen. But even Brother Lawrence observed set times for prayer and Scripture reading, when he gave his total attention to God. (By the way, entire books have been written on the topic of prayer. In this book, I've talked about prayer in a general way. In the Appendix, I have listed a few classic books on prayer. See page 144.)

QUIET TIME: A SPIRITUAL DISCIPLINE

Setting time aside for God takes discipline. Spiritual disciplines are habits, practices, customs, patterns, routines that we cultivate for a spiritual purpose. Every life is held together by a web of habits that have become nearly automatic. We have good reasons for habitually going to work and for dressing before we leave the house. Just as we shower and brush our teeth for a reason (we want friends!), we set aside daily time with God for spiritual reasons. We do not consider someone "legalistic" because they always dress before going out in public. We don't even question the practice. We won't question the habit of meeting with God, either, if we understand its importance.

To love God with all of your being, you must get your mind, body, and emotions all pointing in the same direction. Spiritual disciplines are practices that will help you love God with all of your being.

WHY HAVE A QUIET TIME?

Of all the questions you could ask about quiet time, the most critical is "Why should I have a quiet time?" If you understand *why* a quiet time is important, you will find it easier to establish the practice. Habits practiced without clear purpose soon degenerate into meaningless ritual. It's almost impossible to maintain a discipline for long without sound motivations. There are three basic reasons that form a foundation upon which you can build a lifetime of meetings with God.

REASONS FOR HAVING A QUIET TIME

- God desires to meet with you.
- You need it.
- The world desperately needs to see Christ in you.

God Desires to Meet with You

As incredible as it sounds, the full weight of the Bible supports the idea that God wants to meet with you. He created all that is. He lacks nothing. God has no emotional or psychological needs. He is complete in Himself. But because He is love, He created people to both receive His love and to respond to His love. Love always seeks expression and response.

We know that God is great. He is all-knowing, all-powerful, in control, infinite, and holy. Sometimes as we reflect on His limitless majesty, we forget that He has emotions like ours: God loves (see John 3:16), is deeply moved and troubled (see John 11:33), and weeps (see John 11:35), just to name a few. The emotions we feel, as people made in the image of God, help us identify with the scope of God's emotions.

Before Jesus went to the cross, He agonized over humanity's resistance to His love: "O Jerusalem, Jerusalem, you who kill the prophets and stone those sent to you, how often have I *longed* to gather your children together, as a hen gathers her chicks under her wings, but you were not willing" (Matthew 23:37, emphasis added).

As you come to your quiet time, remember that God longs for deep friendship with you. When you ask, "Why have a quiet time?" and answer, "Because God desires my company," the axis shifts. The time no longer revolves around *you.* The primary issue is no longer "What do I get out of it?" but "How has our relationship been enriched?" You come to this date because God Almighty requests the pleasure of your company. You happily make the effort because He is your God and He wants you to know and love Him.

When you devote time to God, you allow Him to tell you the things He is yearning to tell you. You may keep forgetting how much He loves you; in quiet time, He'll tell you again and again. The God of all that is, both in time and eternity, longs to show Himself to you, to open His heart and mind to you. God wants to bring you into His inner circle, into the boardroom where company strategies are disclosed. Jesus said, "I no longer call you servants, because a servant does not know his master's business. Instead I call you friends, for everything I learned from my Father I have made known to you" (John 15:15).

Of course, God communicates these messages to you all the time, not just during quiet time. The problem is that your life gets busy and blurry. You lose focus. You miss His overtures. God may be knocking Himself out to get your attention, but you forget to look up. Quiet time is His idea to help you refocus. It's His idea, a date for just the two of you.

You Need It

The second reason to have a quiet time is that you need it. You were created for friendship with God. Everything about you finds its fullest expression and satisfaction in relationship with Him. You were created with a capacity for intimate relationship that no human being can fill. You will always feel something is missing in your friendships, career, and leisure activities because they cannot touch that place in you that only God can satisfy.

God created you for a purpose. He has plans for you. But you will never know the fullness of your destiny until you cooperate with His design. You need daily time apart with God to see Him more clearly and to align yourself with His heart and mind. His design and direction for your life is not so much "Go there and do this" as it is "Come near to Me and become like Jesus." This demands time focused on God. He wants to make you the *you* He had in mind when He created you. This *you* can only be formed in His presence. (For more on the benefits of quiet time, see chapter 3.)

The World Desperately Needs to See Christ in You

Some years ago I had what I call a "Vitamin E Night" (E for Encouragement) in our home and invited both believing and unbelieving friends. One neighbor came into the kitchen to speak to me. "Patti has what you have and so does Colleen, but Millie doesn't," she said. This neighbor had not yet come to Christ, but she could identify believers whose lives manifested Christ. The incident reminded me that through His people, Jesus spreads His fragrance to others (see 2 Corinthians 2:14). The fragrance of Christ is radiated from us when we have been in His presence. When Moses came down off the mountain after spending forty days with the Lord, His face shone. He had lingered in God's presence and came away reflecting His glory (see Exodus 34:29-35, 2 Corinthians 3:18).

We live in a needy world—a world that needs to know Christ. God has called us to be light and salt to that world. He wants to bless us that we might be a blessing to others. Quiet time is not an isolated act of devotion estranged from the rest of life. It is an affirmation that we desire to express our devotion to Christ all day long in every endeavor and all our dealings with people.

PREPARE TO MEET YOUR MAKER

Preparation is part of life. We reread notes before giving a presentation. We clean the guest room and fold back the bedcovers to welcome a guest. We gather ingredients or tools before making a soufflé or overhauling the transmission. The Bible mentions that even Jesus is preparing a place for us in heaven (see John 14:2-3).

Preparation speaks volumes, especially in relationships. Last Thanksgiving, for example, our family rendezvoused at our daughter and son-in-law's home to celebrate the holiday. Beth and her children had created pilgrim hats and Indian headdresses for each of us to wear at the meal. Even the five-month-old baby had a hat to wear. When they brought the hats out, we knew we had been planned for. Before we ever arrived, we were in their thoughts; we were important to them. In the same way, we convey our desire to develop a friendship with God by making certain preparations.

My Preparation to Meet with God

☐ I will set apart time to meet with God today, tomorrow, and the rest of the week.

☐ I will meet with the Lord at _____ A.M./P.M.

☐ I will meet with the Lord _____ (location).

☐ I will prepare by gathering a few things to help cultivate my relationship with God:

☐ a Bible

☐ pen and paper (a spiral-bound notebook or a binder work well and help you keep your quiet time notes together)

☐ this book, *Feeding Your Soul: A Quiet Time Handbook*

Each chapter of this book is followed by a suggested application ("Making It Personal"). Use these ideas to help you get started. Then use the reflection/discussion questions (on your own or with others) to further stimulate your thinking and help you establish the practice of meeting with God.

⠿SUMMARY⠿

Quiet time is the portion of your day reserved for you and God alone. Your relationship with God requires time and attention if it is to grow. Three basic reasons should motivate your quiet time: (1) God desires to meet with you, (2) you need this regular time with Him, and (3) you live in a world that desperately needs to see Christ in you.

⠿MAKING IT PERSONAL⠿

Once you have determined a time and place and gathered the supplies you will use in your quiet time, begin to prepare yourself. Quiet your heart. Use the paragraph below to help you focus on God. After you read the following paragraph, stop, close your eyes, and imagine that you are God. Imagine how He feels about you.

You created everything that is, universe after universe. You placed this beautiful, blue planet in orbit and filled it with men, women, and children. You made humans in Your own image so that You could have relationship with them. Everything You made was for Your glory and pleasure. Unfortunately, the people You made are always looking somewhere else, always busy with other things. (Pause and imagine, then continue putting yourself in God's place.)

You try one thing after another to get their attention. You talk to one man from a burning bush, You march people through the Red Sea without getting their feet wet, You give them a book to reveal who You are and what You think. Years later, You even become human and live among them and die for them. Then You rise from the dead and make it possible for them to live forever with You in heaven — all because You desire relationship with them.

Despite all this, for the most part they act as if You don't exist. Or, if You do, it doesn't matter much to real life. You yearn for meaningful contact, but You never force Yourself on anybody. After all, what kind of relationship would that be? You do what You can, and wait.

Begin your quiet time with **silent reflection**. Put yourself in God's place and consider how much He wants you to know Him.

Now, **read** the passages listed for each day. (If you are unfamiliar with the Bible, use the list on page 27 or the one in the front of your

Bible to help you find the New Testament book written by Mark.)
Each of the first four books of the New Testament—Matthew, Mark,
Luke, John—is a biography of Jesus Christ. This week you will be
reading about Christ from the book of Mark.

Day 1: Gospel of Mark, chapter 1, verses 1-8 (Mark 1:1-8)
Day 2: Mark 1:9-20
Day 3: Mark 1:21-34
Day 4: Mark 1:35-45
Day 5: Mark 2:1-12
Day 6: Mark 2:13-22
Day 7: Mark 2:23–Mark 3:6

After you read the section for the day, **write** a note to God in
your quiet time notebook. Express briefly anything you want to say
to God. Write to Him about your current circumstances and your
reading in the Bible.

EXAMPLE

May 14, 1998
Mark 1:1-8
Dear God, I want to begin meeting with You. There's a lot I don't
understand. Please teach me. Just as God sent John to prepare
people to meet Jesus, help me prepare to meet with You.
   I'm concerned about the rumored layoffs and the state of our
finances. I'm anxious and confused. Please help me know what I
should do.

Terrific! You are on your way in life's richest experience. Continue on to the next chapter for more help in developing your
friendship with God.

⁞⁞REFLECTION AND DISCUSSION QUESTIONS⁞⁞

1. How did the exercise of putting yourself in God's place help you prepare your heart to meet with Him?

2. What aspects of having a relationship with God are most meaningful to you currently? His friendship? His comfort? His forgiveness? Something else?

3. Why is a daily meeting alone with God foundational to promoting friendship with Him?

4. Read John 15:15. God wants to be personal and intimate with you. In what ways have you experienced God's friendship this week?

5. Read over the notes you wrote to God this week. What did you learn about God? About yourself?

6. How do you think your times apart with God have affected your other relationships? Your work? Your attitudes this week?

OLD TESTAMENT

Gen.	Genesis
Ex.	Exodus
Lev.	Leviticus
Num.	Numbers
Dt.	Deuteronomy
Josh.	Joshua
Jdg.	Judges
Ruth	Ruth
1 Sam.	1 Samuel
2 Sam.	2 Samuel
1 K.	1 Kings
2 K.	2 Kings
1 Chron.	1 Chronicles
2 Chron.	2 Chronicles
Ezra	Ezra
Neh.	Nehemiah
Est.	Esther
Job	Job
Ps.	Psalms
Prov.	Proverbs
Eccl.	Ecclesiastes
S. of S.	Song of Songs
Is.	Isaiah
Jer.	Jeremiah
Lam.	Lamentations
Ezk.	Ezekiel
Dan.	Daniel
Hos.	Hosea
Joel	Joel
Amos	Amos
Ob.	Obadiah
Jon.	Jonah
Mic.	Micah
Nah.	Nahum
Hab.	Habbakuk
Zeph.	Zephaniah
Hag.	Haggai
Zech.	Zechariah
Mal.	Malachi

NEW TESTAMENT

Mt.	Matthew
Mk.	Mark
Lk.	Luke
Jn.	John
Acts	Acts
Ro.	Romans
1 Cor.	1 Corinthians
2 Cor.	2 Corinthians
Gal.	Galatians
Eph.	Ephesians
Phil.	Philippians
Col.	Colossians
1 Thess.	1 Thessalonians
2 Thess.	2 Thessalonians
1 Tim.	1 Timothy
2 Tim.	2 Timothy
Titus	Titus
Phlm.	Philemon
Heb.	Hebrews
Jas.	James
1 Pet.	1 Peter
2 Pet.	2 Peter
1 Jn.	1 John
2 Jn.	2 John
3 Jn.	3 John
Jude	Jude
Rev.	Revelation

TWO

The Nuts and Bolts of Quiet Time

QUIET TIME WITH GOD IS A CALLING, A JOY, AND A PRIVILEGE, which Jesus Christ made possible through His death. But you may be wondering what exactly you *do* in a quiet time. Good question. If the idea of having a date with God sounds wonderful and mysterious but raises questions in your mind, you're not alone. Early in my experience as a new believer, I heard people speak of a quiet time with God without ever clarifying what they meant or how to do it. Most of us need either a model or clear instructions. This chapter deals with the practical aspects of keeping an appointment with God.

WHEN?

Start now. As with most things in life, there never seems to be a *good* time to institute a new habit. Perhaps you're a student adjusting to college, juggling a heavy semester, or facing the deadline of a major paper. Or maybe you have a new job or a new baby or health problems or some other situation. The temptation is to delay, to wait for a more convenient time to begin having a quiet time. But the ideal time may never come. Most worthwhile practices become part of our lives only if we make real effort under less than perfect conditions.

C. S. Lewis wrote, "The only people who achieve much are those who want knowledge so badly that they seek it while the conditions are still unfavourable. Favourable conditions never come."[1]

Forming a beneficial habit can be hard work, but it's worth the trouble. The sooner you establish the practice of quiet time, the sooner the habit can serve you. Suppose that every morning when the alarm goes off you must decide whether or not you'll turn off the alarm, how to turn it off, when you'll turn it off, which hand you'll use, whether to turn it off from bed or from a standing position, and so on. You would never make it out of bed! You make progress in the more important things of life because many of the simpler operations are nearly automatic. A thoughtfully formed habit enables you to spend time shaping your life according to what you understand God's will to be. Oswald Chambers wrote, "Routine is God's way of saving us between our times of inspiration."[2]

So start as soon as possible, and commit yourself to quiet time every day. Why every day? Because you are a drifter and a forgetter. Left to yourself you will stray off course. The current doesn't stop, so you've got to keep rowing—daily.

Begin with a wholehearted, rigorous commitment. Boldly say, "Lord, I want to keep an appointment with You every day for the rest of my life. I will start meeting with You today, and I plan to meet with You tomorrow and the next day and the day after that."

This approach has great advantage over dribbling into the habit by, say, a commitment to meet with God three out of seven days a week this year and five out of seven next year. A halting, tentative approach to establishing a habit is like trying to coax a donkey up a flight of stairs. Take a bold step forward. Make daily time with the Lord a priority. Studies show that a new habit can be well established in less than a month if you do it every day.

Aim for every day and learn from the days when you miss your quiet time. If you consistently miss on Wednesdays, you may realize that your Tuesday night meeting puts you to bed later than usual or that you have breakfast with someone on Wednesday mornings that keeps you from your quiet time. Once you've identified the issue, you may be able to figure out a way to work around it. Don't let missed days defeat you. Learn from them. Commitment breeds creativity. Decide to make quiet times alone with God part of your life, and you'll find a way even in the swirl of life.

Let's continue probing the question of "When?" Although the Bible doesn't prescribe a particular time to meet with God, I suggest as early in your day as possible for strictly practical reasons. It seems wise to fortify your spirit, reset the compass of your heart, and renew your mind before striking out to meet the uncertain day. David said, "In the morning, O Lord, you hear my voice; in the morning I lay my requests before you and wait in expectation" (Psalm 5:3).

God invited Moses to meet with Him this way: "Be ready in the morning, and then come up on Mt. Sinai. Present yourself to me there on the top of the mountain"(Exodus 34:2). This passage is a good model for quiet time for several reasons. "Be ready" reminds us to prepare for our time with God. "In the morning" encourages us to focus our eyes on the Lord as we begin a new day. "Present yourself," as it's used here in the Hebrew, is to station yourself before God.

Although I encourage you to set apart time with God as early in your day as possible, when it comes right down to it, any time is a good time. The Bible records incidents of men and women drawing aside to spend time alone with the Lord at every conceivable time of the day and night. About 2,500 years ago, it was Daniel's practice to have his quiet time at three appointed times every day: "Now when Daniel learned that the decree had been published, he went home to his upstairs room where the windows opened toward Jerusalem. Three times a day he got down on his knees and prayed, giving thanks to his God, just as he had done before" (Daniel 6:10). Throughout his life, the writer of Psalm 119 met with the Lord at various times: at midnight to give thanks (Psalm 119:62), before dawn to cry for help (verse 147), throughout the night to meditate on God's promises (verse 148), and even seven times a day to give God praise (verse 164). Whew!

Louise was a new follower of Jesus Christ when we began to meet together. We talked about the importance of spending time with the Lord each day and shared what we were learning about God and ourselves. I remember Louise asking one day, "Is it all right to have a quiet time morning and evening?"

Of course! The morning and evening pattern reminds us that

God instituted a morning and evening sacrifice (see Exodus 29:39). Our Lord met with His Father mornings (see Mark 1:35) and evenings (see Matthew 14:23, Luke 21:37).

Lorne, a mature believer, has made this his pattern for years. In the morning, part of his quiet time is spent praying through that day's schedule and "do list." He asks for wisdom and strength, sensitivity and boldness, as he considers the people and tasks he will face that day. In the evening, he prays through the day backward. As he considers his day, Lorne prays for the people he talked with, reviews their conversations, and notes any actions he is to take.

The answer to the question "When?" is that *any time* is a good time to meet with your Maker. Consider your particular circumstances, set a time for your daily quiet time, and begin today.

WHERE?

Ideally, you might choose a majestic cathedral, a mountain top, or a leather chair by a crackling fire for your appointment with God, but this isn't an ideal world. Men and women have met with God in dank prison cells and from beds of pain. Suzanna Wesley, mother of nineteen children, flipped her apron over her head and prayed in the midst of her busy household. My husband, Roger, met with God in the latrine during Army bootcamp. My friend Yori prayed while sitting cross-legged on her bed with a large, black shawl tented over her, blocking out the comings and goings of her roommates.

Throughout your life you may meet with the Lord in many varied places determined by your circumstances. Leni spreads her Bible and notebook on her bed and kneels there to read and pray. Jean rests her Bible on the arm of the rocking chair and meets with God as she nurses her baby. Alan meets with God in his car in the parking lot at work. John sits at the kitchen table; he likes a firm chair and a good writing surface. His wife Pat prefers to prop up in bed with her Bible and notebook. My husband likes to go to the same place morning after morning. If we are away from home, he determines the night before where he will meet with the Lord and returns to that place as long as we are there.

In his book, *A Serious Call to a Devout and Holy Life*, William

Law (1686–1761) recommends that, if possible, we always have our prayer time in the same place. He encouraged keeping that place for the sole purpose of prayer and Bible reading. Law felt that by consecrating a place, we would go there with an increased reverence. The Bible says of the patriarch Abraham: "Early the next morning Abraham got up and returned to the place where he had stood before the LORD" (Genesis 19:27). To meet with God where He has met with you before is a powerful experience.

HOW LONG?

How long you spend in quiet time is to a large extent a matter of your spiritual appetite. Start small—try ten minutes a day—but be consistent. Consistency is more important than the length of time. The goal is not to read through the Bible in a year or to spend an hour a day in prayer. You are coming to your quiet time to meet with your Lord, to give Him your undivided attention because He loves you and you love Him. Keep in mind that you are cultivating a practice for a spiritual purpose: God desires your friendship; you want to know and love God; the world desperately needs to see Christ in you.

Many people have started a lifelong practice of quiet time with only a small chunk of time. Most people who regularly meet with the Lord find that this time becomes the highlight of their day. Ten minutes expands because the blessings and benefits are so great.

HOW?

As you've already noticed, there aren't set rules for quiet time. This is a time to cultivate a relationship with God, and relationships are personal and ever-changing. My times with God will look different from yours, and my times with God will look different at various periods in my life. Personality, circumstances, stage of life, spiritual maturity, and appetite all affect our life with Christ.

Scattered throughout the book are examples of how people spend their dates with God. These examples will give you ideas and remind you that your time with the Lord is personal and unique.

BASIC ELEMENTS: GOD'S WORD AND PRAYER

There aren't set rules for quiet time, but there are basic elements. Communication is critical to any relationship. In your times alone with God, He speaks to you and you speak to Him. God has revealed Himself most fully through the Bible. In it, He tells who He is; what He is like; and what He thinks, values, and hates. God tells you what He is doing in the world and how you fit into His plans. God details in the Bible the riches that are yours because you belong to Christ, and He makes plain how He wants you to live. The Bible is a love letter written to you from a God who is always making ways for you to draw near to Him.

Reading God's Word is essential. Why? Because we want to hear from God—we want to hear truth. Without regular interaction with the Scriptures, we can't be sure that we're hearing from God. Bible reading reveals God, transforms minds, and nourishes spirits.

Conversations are two-sided: give and take. God speaks to you through His Word and by His Spirit, and you respond to Him through prayer. Sometimes you initiate the subject and then listen to hear what He will say to you. Sometimes God initiates the subject as you read from the Bible, and you respond to Him in prayer.

This morning, for example, I was reading Isaiah 55:10-11: "As the rain and the snow come down from heaven, and do not return to it without watering the earth and making it bud and flourish, so that it yields seed for the sower and bread for the eater, so is my word that goes out from my mouth: It will not return to me empty, but will accomplish what I desire and achieve the purpose for which I sent it."

As I read this passage in the Bible, *God* initiated the topic of conversation—His Word. Thoughts and questions came to my mind: *God's Word is like rain and snow—refreshing, nourishing. Do I believe that His words come to me as miraculous gifts from heaven? Do I realize that just as God rained down manna on the children of Israel, He is raining down spiritual nourishment for me? Do I believe that God's Word can make me fruitful?* I responded in prayer: "Lord, thank You for Your Word, which You have sent to accomplish Your will on earth. Help me to open my heart more fully to Your Word so that it may achieve Your desired purpose in my life."

Or *I* might initiate the conversation. I express my concerns to God: "Lord, I'm concerned about Susie. Help me know how to think about the situation." I begin reading the Bible. God may speak through the passage I am reading or He may bring to mind thoughts from another portion of the Bible. The Holy Spirit, our teacher, suggests the implications and applications of the Bible to specific situations. Implications suggest the meanings and outcomes of a passage of Scripture to a specific situation. Applications deal with practical outworkings of a passage in our lives.

For example, Isaiah 55:10-11 teaches that God's Word will accomplish His purposes on earth. I ask, "Lord, what is the significance of this verse to Susie's situation? I know that You use Your Word to minister to Your people on earth. Please send Your Word to accomplish Your purposes in Susie's life. Lord, You often use people to minister Your Word to others. Is there anything You want me to do to touch Susie's life for Your purposes?"

The application might be to *pray* that the Word would fall like rain on Susie to refresh and encourage her, or to *share* something with Susie from my time with God.

A PLAN

Quiet time has no set rules, but you do need a plan. Without some kind of blueprint, you will tend to wander aimlessly through your quiet time. Your plan grows out of your purpose: to keep company with God and to get to know Him, to worship and obey Him, and to be changed by Him.

Here are several plans. Choose one for this week. Stick with that plan until you feel ready to move on, then try another or add new elements to what you currently are doing. Throughout this book you will glean ideas from others. These ideas and insights can help you keep your quiet time fresh and vital.

Plan A

Prepare your heart. Tell God you've come to meet with Him.

Today, as you continue reading in the gospel of Mark, begin to mark your Bible. Use colored pencils or a highlighter pen to emphasize what seems important to you. Or use a pen to underline or circle meaningful words or phrases. The idea is to engage yourself more fully as you read and to make portions stand out so that you can return to them.

Continue to write notes to God in your quiet time notebook.

Plan B

Our early education was defined by the "Three Rs": reading, 'riting and 'rithmetic. This quiet time plan is outlined by the "Four Rs": *read, report, reflect*, and *respond*. Here's how this plan works.

Read. Choose a book of the Bible and read a portion each morning until you finish that book. Then choose another book of the Bible to read through. I would suggest you start with the gospel of Mark, then read Philippians. The amount you read is up to you. Some mornings one verse may occupy your entire time. At other times, you may read a larger chunk (probably not more than a chapter). Read slowly and thoughtfully. At the top of the page of your quiet time notebook, record the date and the reference of the passage you read.

Report. In your notebook, make notes about what you read. Record the facts. Summarize the content. The idea is to engage yourself with what God has written to you. At this point, you are a reporter—be objective. Do not interpret what you read.

Reflect. Consider the facts. What do they mean? What do you learn about God from this passage? How will that make a difference for you today? What does God say about you? How does that change your outlook? Are there any commands or instructions in this portion of Scripture? How might you apply them today? (View the reflection questions as stimulation to your meditation, not an assignment. The objective is to commune with God, not to answer the questions.)

Respond. Talk to God. Let your reflection inspire your prayer. Tell God what you saw about Him that you appreciate (that's praise). Thank Him for what He has done for you. Ask for His help as you seek to obey what He shows you.

Here are three examples of how this plan looks. If you are just beginning to meet with God, your quiet time may look something like the first example. The second and third examples are more complete. Depending on how much time you set aside, the passage of Scripture itself and the insights God gives you, the amount you write will vary.

Example 1 (shorter version)

April 14, 1997

Read: Matthew 6:28-34

Report: Jesus tells His followers not to worry and to seek Him first.

Reflect: Jesus says don't worry, but seek Him first. "But" has the idea of instead of.

Respond: Lord, I can see that meeting with You before I go to work really diminishes my worry level. Please help me seek You first in everything I do today.

Example 2 (longer version)

July 7, 1997

Read: Mark 1:35-39

Report: After a busy day and probably a late night, Jesus got up while it was still dark to meet with His Father. He chose a solitary place. His friends came looking for Him. They said everyone was looking for Him. He said that they would go to the nearby villages to preach and they did.

Reflect: Jesus paid a price to meet with His Father. It probably wasn't easy to get up early after such a busy day. If Jesus thought it was important for Him, how much more so for me.

People crowded Jesus life. He looked for a private place where He could get some uninterrupted time alone. Where can I go to be alone?

His friends seem to be suggesting that He drop everything and return to minister to the people whom He healed the night before. Even Jesus had people suggesting what He should be doing. Interesting that Jesus did something very different.

To move on when there were opportunities right where He was doesn't seem strategic. How did He decide to go to other towns? Had He received fresh instruction from the Father during His alone time?

Respond: Father, I know that You want to lead me just like You led the Lord Jesus. Direct my path today. Help me to hear Your voice and not just the voices of the people around me. I want to meet with You like Jesus did. Teach me and lead me.

Example 3 (longer version)

October 4, 1997

Read: Daniel 6:1-10

Report: Daniel is in a tough spot. He has been immensely successful in his job as a high political official and this has stirred jealousy among 120 satraps (whatever satraps are). They seek to charge Daniel with some impropriety, but his character and work are impeccable. They figure his devotion to God is his vulnerable point, so they convince the king to issue an edict. This new law says that anyone who prays to any god besides the king will be thrown into the lions den.

"Now when Daniel learned that the decree had been published, he went home to his upstairs room where the windows opened toward Jerusalem. Three times a day he got down on his knees and prayed, giving thanks to his God, just as he had done before."

Reflect: Daniel had a great reason not to have his quiet time. What helped him to be faithful?

He had an established pattern: a place, a time, a plan.

Respond: Lord, forgive me for letting such small things keep me from meeting with You. My life has never been threatened for having a quiet time. Please help me lay a strong foundation of setting apart time for just the two of us so that when tough times come I'll be faithful to You.

▓▓SUMMARY▓▓

Begin today to meet daily with the Lord. Any time is good for a quiet time, but start as early in your day as possible. Choose a place. Follow a plan. Keep the purpose of quiet time in mind.

▓▓MAKING IT PERSONAL▓▓

☐ Tell the Lord you want to meet with Him daily for the rest of your life.

☐ Determine when: _____ A.M./P.M.

☐ Decide where: _____

☐ Follow one of the plans suggested in this chapter during your meeting with the Lord.

▓▓REFLECTION AND DISCUSSION QUESTIONS▓▓

1. Consider these quotes:

> "The only people who achieve much are those who want knowledge so badly that they seek it while the conditions are still unfavourable. Favourable conditions never come."
>
> —C. S. Lewis

> "Commitment breeds creativity. Decide to make quiet times alone with God a part of your life and you'll find a way even in the swirl of life." (page 30)

What circumstances make this a less than ideal time for you to practice the habit of meeting alone with the Lord each day?

What creative solutions might help you be successful? Did you miss any days of quiet time last week? What did you learn from missed days that will help you in the future?

2. What do you think are the most important elements for building a new habit into your life? What specific steps might you institute?

3. What are the advantages of having a quiet time early in the day?

4. This chapter mentioned the quiet times of some biblical figures and some contemporary believers. Which examples were encouraging, challenging, or instructive for you? In what ways?

5. Share something from your quiet time this week with your discussion group or with a friend.

THREE

What Quiet Time Can Do for You

A YOUNG WOMAN FROM ANOTHER COUNTRY TOLD ME THAT WHEN she came to this country, she was offended that she was referred to as an *alien*. Up until then she had only heard the term used to describe someone from outer space. I laughed.

Perhaps it will come as a shock to you that if you are a true believer in Jesus Christ, the Bible calls *you* an alien. Peter calls believers "aliens and strangers in the world" (1 Peter 2:11). When you came to personal faith in Christ, you became a child of God and began to live between two worlds—this one on earth and your eternal home in heaven. Jesus said that you are no longer of this world any more than He is (see John 17:14-16). Nevertheless, He leaves you on earth to fulfill His purposes. But while you live here physically, God tells you to fix your eyes on the real but invisible life you have with Christ.

God has "blessed us in the heavenly realms with every spiritual blessing in Christ" (Ephesians 1:3). How do we as aliens keep our attention on the spiritual realms — the unseen things above—when the seen world is glittering around us? How do we as strangers and pilgrims maneuver on earth while keeping our eyes on heaven? To navigate this challenging terrain, we need to fix our eyes on the truths of God every day.

BENEFITS OF QUIET TIME

Quiet time is a place filled with benefits where we can fix our eyes on God and the invisible realities of our lives. Take a look at just some of those benefits.

Quiet Time Is Your "Extricating" Place.

Have you ever stood at the ocean's edge and felt the surge of incoming waves and the pull of retreating water around your legs? Perhaps the roar and swoosh, the surge and pull, the radiance of spray, and the taste of salt held you in a hypnotic trance for several minutes. When you came to your senses you realized that the sand had formed strong, sucking mouths around your ankles. It took effort to extricate yourself. Remember?

It's the same in your spiritual life. If you stand still, the sediment of the world builds up around you and causes you to sink. Unfortunately, you may be lulled into a false sense of well-being while you sink deeper in the mire.

Life on this planet is full of challenges for the Christian alien. The world is familiar, comfortable, and natural to you, but it is hostile to your faith in Christ. Although God has redeemed you from this world and drawn you into His kingdom, you tend to drift, to stray away from your first love for Christ. This happens subtly. All you need to do is *nothing*, and the world will suck you back under its influence.

Quiet Time Is Your "Renewing" Place.

God calls you to live by faith. This means believing and acting with confidence based on unseen realities (see Hebrews 11:1). All the while, the visible, tangible world exerts its neon gravitational pull. You don't intend for it to happen, but the compass of your soul is pulled off true north as you trod along. The Bible strongly warns and urges you: "Do not conform any longer to the pattern of this world, but be transformed by the renewing of your mind. Then you will be able to test and approve what God's will is—his good, pleasing and perfect will" (Romans 12:2).

God calls you to preside over the care of your soul so that it is not squeezed into the world's mold. He wants you to actively engage in reshaping your mind according to His truth. Renew your mind. Then you can live by faith, not sight.

Quiet Time Is a "Setting" Place.

Jesus, too, lived in a world hostile and foreign to what He knew in heaven. Although it was a world He created, it neither recognized nor received Him (see John 1:10-11). During the years Jesus lived on earth, He lived attached to the Father and the eternal reality He knew from experience. He stayed connected to what He knew through His communion with the Father; we stay attached to a reality we know by faith in the same way. "Since, then, you have been raised with Christ, set your hearts on things above, where Christ is seated at the right hand of God. Set your minds on things above, not on earthly things. For you died, and your life is now hidden with Christ in God" (Colossians 3:1-3).

Set your heart. Set your mind.

Quiet Time Is Your "Identity-Shaping" Place.

Living between two worlds can create an identity crisis. Who will tell you who you are? If you form your conception of who you are from the feedback you receive from the world, you will be accepting misinformation. Don't look to others to assign value to you, to tell you how you fit into the scheme of things. They can't. Only the God who created and redeemed you can tell you who you are, why you're here, and where you're going.

In the movie *My Fair Lady*, Eliza Doolittle is transformed from a poor cockney flower girl into a glamorous, cultured woman. Many books and movies are based on the idea that there is a prince inside our froggy selves. One of the reasons we respond to that idea is because it is rooted in truth. The Bible teaches that you are a new creation in Christ (see 2 Corinthians 5:17). But your new self doesn't emerge singing "The Rain in Spain" or burst forth after a princess's kiss. Although you may still look pretty much the same, something very real happened deep inside you when you trusted your life to Jesus Christ. Whatever happened to you when you believed in Christ means that you can never fully be your old self again.

This is why quiet time is so important. God is the only one who can tell you who you are because He designed you in the womb and He gave you second birth in Jesus Christ. Just as physical birth is merely the beginning, so spiritual birth is a starting point from which to grow, learn, and develop. In Christ you have a new identity. The trouble is that as you scuff along here on earth, you easily forget that God has chosen you and changed you (see John 15:16, Ephesians 1:4) and that you are a citizen of heaven (see Philippians 3:20).

Quiet Time Is Your "Remembering" Place.

You need to be reminded every day that God loves you (see Ephesians 2:4), that His plans for you are good (see Jeremiah 29:11), and that He will never leave you or forsake you (see Hebrews 13:5). Consider His death in your place and His desire for you to live with Him in heaven forever—and marvel.

> The LORD your God is with you, he is mighty to save.
> He will take great delight in you, he will quiet you with
>   his love,
> he will rejoice over you with singing. (Zephaniah 3:17)

Quiet Time Is Your "Reason for Existing" Place.

You were created for fellowship with God. The words *salvation* and *blessing*, which pop up everywhere in the Bible, burst with the promise of good coming to you because you belong to Jesus Christ. You were created for a wholeness that you cannot know apart from relationship with God. David expressed it this way: "You have made known to me the path of life; you will fill me with joy in your presence, with eternal pleasures at your right hand" (Psalm 16:11).

Quiet Time Is Your "Knowing God" Place.

When Jesus Christ appeared to Paul on the road to Damascus, Paul asked, "Who are you, Lord?" What a great question—a question that only God can answer. Because God is invisible, eternal, infinite, and holy, we are dependent on His revelation of Himself. Our notion of God must be shaped by what He says about Himself or else we create a god in our own minds, which is as much an idol as one carved from wood or stone. A. W. Tozer wrote:

It is impossible to keep our moral practices sound and our inward attitudes right while our idea of God is erroneous or inadequate. If we would bring back spiritual power to our lives, we must begin to think of God more nearly as He is.[1]

Quiet Time Is Your "Intimacy with God" Place.

Day after day, God answers the question "Who are you, Lord?" for Sam, a businessman in California. Sam's dad died when he was only nine years old, but Sam's memory of his dad is clear. Beside Sam's bed is a photo of his dad cradling Sam, then nine months old, in his arms. Just as that photo captures for Sam the intimacy between a human father and his child, quiet time helps Sam form an accurate picture of God as his Father. And Sam isn't merely accumulating information about God as Father. He is learning to walk through life with his hand in his heavenly Father's hand. It is one thing to recite "Our Father" at the beginning of a prayer; it is another to *experience* God as Father: providing, protecting, comforting, instructing, disciplining, and tucking us in at night.

Like Sam, Joyce has a history of very personal experiences with the Lord. Morning after morning she goes to the kitchen and puts on the coffee. While she waits for the coffee to brew, she feeds the chickens. Then, with coffee in hand, she climbs the stairs to her room and sits in her cone-shaped Papasan chair. On the floor is a stack of Bibles in various translations and *Daily Light*, a hundred-year-old devotional book containing Scripture selections with no commentary. She reads, prays, and writes to preserve her thoughts from this time.

One morning, Joyce came to her time with God feeling an overwhelming sense of her unworthiness. She was experiencing "post-traumatic-stress" symptoms again, symptoms that often recur in people who have faced extreme emotional suffering. Feelings of guilt, unfounded but powerful, surrounded her. The weight of sorrow and helplessness oppressed her. Her despair was so great that she wondered how she could even ask God for His help. But the practice of meeting with God was an established part of her life. Joyce knew where to run when heaviness comes like a flood. She began to read in the devotional book she had used for years. As she opened to that day's selection, she felt a strong urge to turn back to the reading for the previous morning. When she flipped back, her eyes settled on the verse, "Woman, where are your accusers?" (John 8:10). In this intimate, personal exchange, God spoke to her deep need and set her free from self-accusation.

Every day in quiet time you can weave another thread into the fabric of your life with God. Bring the thread, which represents your needs, concerns, and dreams, to the Weaver's loom where God creates a tapestry of experiences you share with Him. As Bible teacher Jim Downing has said, "How well we know God is in direct proportion to the number and depth of shared experiences."

Quiet Time Is Your "Beholding and Molding" Place.

Quiet time reminds you that God intends for you to become like Jesus Christ (see Romans 8:29). It is not only possible for you to be changed, it is imperative. In fact, if you are not different since your "conversion," perhaps you have not yet come to true faith in Jesus Christ. Woven into the warp and woof of life in Christ is the assumption of change. A changed life is the validation of your encounter with God. This change doesn't happen all at once or without accompanying failures, but authentic change is inherent in our life with Christ.

Change takes place as we focus our attention on Christ and reflect His likeness. "And we, who with unveiled faces all reflect the Lord's glory, are being transformed into his likeness with ever-increasing glory, which comes from the Lord, who is the Spirit" (2 Corinthians 3:18). Change also occurs as we consciously obey the teachings of Christ. As He reveals His will, seek to do it. Twelfth-century monk St. Bernard of Clairvaux comments on this idea:

> His features we see not; and yet they mold us, not by
> their outward beauty striking on our bodily sight, but by
> the love and joy they kindle in our hearts.[2]

Quiet Time Is Your "Puttin' Off and Puttin' On" Place.
God tells you to put off the old person and put on the new (see Ephesians 4:22-24). This is a process, like undressing and dressing, that must be done on a spiritual level over and over again. In quiet time, you'll often discover that some old rag you thought you had discarded long ago is slung around your shoulders again. God makes you aware that you're wearing an old attitude or that you've slipped back into practices contrary to your new life as a follower of Christ. Your daily time with the Lord helps you slip out of the old, tattered, and soiled garment and don your new clean life in Christ again.

Quiet Time Is Your "Food and Fellowship" Place.
Time with the Lord is soul food, necessary for the life and satisfaction of your soul. Books with the word "soul" in the title have been hot sellers recently. People sense a hunger for something that can touch their essence. But unless a book on the care of the soul calls the reader to come to Jesus and His Word, it cannot keep its promise. The prophet Isaiah records God's warning and invitation: "Why spend money on what is not bread, and your labor on what does not satisfy? Listen, listen to me, and eat what is good, and your soul will delight in the richest of fare. Give ear and come to me; hear me, that your soul may live. I will make an everlasting covenant with you, my faithful love promised to David" (Isaiah 55:2-3).

A tasty, attractively presented meal shared with friends is one of life's true pleasures. A good meal in good company is a taste of what God wants for your soul. Quiet time is fellowship with God over the delicious and nourishing fare of His Word. When the Lord says, "your soul will delight in the richest of fare," He tells you to come to Him and listen to Him. You need to *hear* God's words spoken to you if you are to experience joy in your deepest places. No wonder Jeremiah said, "When your words came, I ate them; they were my joy and my heart's delight" (Jeremiah 15:16). Remember, man does not live on bread alone.

Quiet Time Is Your "Listening" Place.
Quiet time is a scheduled time with God designed to slow you down, to make you pause, to quiet the constant chatter long enough

that you might hear the still voice of God. When you fall silent, God has the opportunity to get a word in edgewise and ask some tough questions. For example, sometimes because you *know* a Bible truth, you think you're obeying it. But you can read about humility, do a Bible study on humility, be able to answer questions about humility, even give a sermon on humility, and *not be humble*. Stop. Hush. Lean forward and listen. Give God room to expose pride in your life. Quiet time is an opportunity for you to hear God speak and make adjustments.

Quiet Time Is Your "Refocusing" Place.

Quiet time can keep you from frittering away your life on the extraneous, the peripheral. In a culture that exalts and feeds busyness, quiet time can refocus your attention daily on what really matters. God will remind you that your relationship with Him is supreme; everything else must be subordinate to that relationship. When you pause in God's presence, the fog clears and values sharpen. You realign yourself with the commitments you've made to God and others. The important things emerge and the secondary things recede once again. The busier you are, the more desperately you need the pause that refreshes.

Quiet Time Is Your "Repenting and Rejoicing" Place.

I have read about compunction in old books but never hear the word used in modern sermons. Too bad. If this word makes you think of acupuncture, it should. It means to prick or pierce. God faithfully administers sharp pokes to make you aware of sin in your life and to prod you to do something about it. These painful jabs are a wake-up call. Compunction is a grace that touches you with sorrow over your sins and moves you to action. In the process, God always assures you of His love as you directly face your sin. Compunction helps you see your sin in relation to God and not just to yourself and other people. God's prodding leads to true repentance.

> *For the word of God is living and active. Sharper than any double-edged sword, it penetrates even to dividing soul and spirit, joints and marrow; it judges the thoughts and attitudes of the heart.* (Hebrews 4:12)

In quiet time, God makes you aware of your sin and gives you hope. Satan is the accuser of believers (see Revelation 12:10). When he points out your sin, he leads you to despair. In Christ you see your sin and mourn. You repent and receive forgiveness and joy. It is a glorious sequence: sin, piercing, remorse, repentance, rejoicing!

Quiet Time Is Your "Healing" Place.
Humans have been called the "walking wounded." All of us take a battering from time to time and need the healing touch of our Lord. In times of pain, confusion, and anguish, King David knew to retreat into God's presence. In 2 Samuel 12, God sent word that David's young son, who was conceived in an adulterous relationship with Bathsheba, was going to die. David, in great agony of spirit, fasted and prayed. He laid on the floor for seven days and prayed that God might spare the child. But when this son died, everyone noticed something strange. David got up off the floor, washed, changed his clothes, worshiped God, ate, and comforted his wife.

Those who observed this were astonished. They asked, "Why are you acting this way? While the child was alive, you fasted and wept, but now that the child is dead, you get up and eat!"

The explanation lies with God's healing power. When David secluded himself in God's presence, he received forgiveness for his sin. He gained an eternal perspective regarding his son's death. He was fortified in his faith so that he was able to trust God in a painful loss. He experienced the grace of God and the balm of God's comfort and strength to offer solace to his grieving wife.

I have friends whose daughter took her own life, friends whose son was murdered, friends who experienced sexual abuse, friends whose teenage son died of cancer. Excruciating pain won't yield to easy answers or clichés. For my friends, the ongoing process of healing began and continues in God's presence.

Quiet Time Is a Place of "Peace and Perspective."
When you spend time with God, He enables you to rethink your life. He lifts your eyes beyond your circumstance to His Person, promises, and perspective. Trouble is part of life on earth, but Jesus has overcome the world (see John 16:33).

Some years ago our family experienced a series of home bur-glaries. In my time with the Lord, He helped me see this unsettling situation in light of His character and care. As I considered the bur-glaries under the warm beam of His love, power, and sovereignty, these troubling episodes led me into a peaceful surrender to the God I knew I could trust. (See Appendix for the quiet time exercise that gave me peace in the midst of this situation.)

Quiet Time Is a "Hope-Reviving" Place.

Don's appearance of robust health is deceiving. In recent years he has faced various times of illness. Yet even in sickness, Don exudes confidence in God. He writes: "If our quiet time is established, we come to God in hope rather than crisis. The quiet time not only gives balance, but also hope that is renewed every day, because God knows and cares." He's right. Hope is a cultivated blessing. Regu-lar contact with a great God gives us stamina and courage to weather hard times.

Quiet Time Is Your "Only Sure Relationship" Place.

The marriage vow has never guaranteed happiness or durability. Many forfeit their promise of faithfulness to their partner. Business contracts are annulled in legal high-stepping. Mothers and fathers deny natural affection for their children and neglect and abuse those given to their care. This world is a precarious and unsure place. If you put your confidence in people, social structures, or the legal sys-tem, you find that the footing inevitably gives way. Even if you are blessed with honorable and godly human relationships, you may outlive them. Nothing and no one can promise to be there for you always. God is the only one who can keep that promise.

Quiet Time Is Your "Question-Asking" Place.

Bill had questions. Lots of them. Over years of enduring a long and painful illness, Bill prayed, "Lord, what do You want me to learn from this? What is the purpose of pain? How do You want me to respond?" Bill asked his pastor and friends for their insights. But most of all, Bill asked God his questions. At Bill's memorial service, several people mentioned his pattern of asking and seeking in the midst of his pain.

Other friends take their questions to God, as well:

- Beth wonders what is the best way to handle sibling rivalry.
- Joanna desires to have a perfect heart. What does that look like?
- Kevin asks what the Bible teaches about employer-employee relationships.

In quiet time, you can ask your questions. God intends for the circumstances of your life to lead you into deeper interaction with Him. He wants your questions and struggles to drive you in His direction. What are you facing? What questions do you have about life? Pray, "Open my eyes that I might see wonderful things in your law" (Psalm 119:18). He delights in answering this prayer. Once you ask, lean toward God in anticipation. Read the Bible in His presence and listen to what His Spirit might say to you.

Your questions may surface from your Bible reading. "What does it mean 'to abide'?" "How do I grow in grace?" Jesus promised, "Ask and it will be given to you; seek and you will find; knock and the door will be opened to you. For everyone who asks receives; he who seeks finds; and to him who knocks, the door will be opened" (Matthew 7:7-8).

Here's an example of how this works. Jesus presented a parable to a crowd at the water's edge. (Parables are terse little stories that make a salient point. They are short and memorable, but their meaning doesn't readily float to the surface.) Even Jesus' disciples, who had heard Him preach many times, often didn't get the point. Although His disciples weren't especially perceptive, they demonstrated some spiritual initiative. After the crowds left, His puzzled disciples came to Jesus to *ask the meaning* of the parables. He told them: "The secret of the kingdom of God has been given to you" (Mark 4:11), and He explained the meaning in simple terms. Spiritual truth is revealed to those who seek it. Asking, seeking, and knocking imply time, effort, and persistence. Once the disciples asked the Lord for the meaning, they had to stick around long enough to hear His answer.

Make your quiet time a place where you withdraw with God to ask your questions about life and His teachings. Ask. Seek. Knock. And then hang around to listen. The answers may not come all at once. It pleases God that you are turning to Him, asking Him to help you make sense of life.

I think you get the idea. We could go on and on. The benefits of quiet time are more numerous than can be mentioned here. Regularly scheduled time alone with God will do more to keep an alien on track and connected to God than any other thing. Make space in your life for daily, personal, alone time with God.

⊞SUMMARY⊞

Quiet time helps spiritual aliens keep their gaze sharply focused on Christ and His kingdom so that they may live between two worlds, serving the kingdom of God on earth. These pilgrims need continual, intense contact with their true, though unseen, life to keep the sand from building up around their ankles. Greatest delight is found in consistent meetings with God. This, after all, is what we aliens were made for.

⊞MAKING IT PERSONAL⊞

- Continue meeting with the Lord using a plan of your choice. You may want to adjust your plan to incorporate new ideas.
- Make "asking, seeking, knocking" part of your daily time. Ask God, verbally or in writing, about your questions and concerns. Then, like the disciples, stick around. Lean toward God in expectation.

- Watch for His answer. Often the answer comes over time, unfolding layer after layer. Keep alert and engaged. Jot insights as they come.
- Remember to thank Him for each layer of answer.

▓▓REFLECTION AND DISCUSSION QUESTIONS▓▓

1. Which benefits of quiet time listed below were most meaningful to you? Describe your need and/or your experience.

☐ Quiet time is your "extricating" place.
☐ Quiet time is your "renewing" place.
☐ Quiet time is a "setting" place.
☐ Quiet time is your "identity-shaping" place.
☐ Quiet time is your "remembering" place.
☐ Quiet time is your "reason for existing" place.
☐ Quiet time is your "knowing God" place.
☐ Quiet time is your "intimacy with God" place.
☐ Quiet time is your "beholding and molding" place.
☐ Quiet time is your "puttin' off and puttin' on" place.
☐ Quiet time is your "food and fellowship" place.
☐ Quiet time is your "listening" place.
☐ Quiet time is your "refocusing" place.
☐ Quiet time is your "repenting and rejoicing" place.
☐ Quiet time is your "healing" place.
☐ Quiet time is a place of "peace and perspective."
☐ Quiet time is your "hope-reviving" place.
☐ Quiet time is your "only sure relationship" place.
☐ Quiet time is your "question-asking" place.

2. How does recognizing that you are an alien deepen your resolve to meet with God daily?

3. What issues or needs stimulated you to "ask, seek, and knock" this week? What have you gained?

4. Jim Downing says, "How well we know God is in direct proportion to the number and depth of shared experiences." How has your quiet time fostered greater intimacy with God this week?

5. Read over the past week's quiet time entries in your notebook. Choose one idea to think on more deeply and to share with the group or a friend.

FOUR

Making Space in Your Life for God

Y OU HAVE SOMETHING IN COMMON WITH THE QUEEN OF ENG-
land, Michael Jordan, the top neuro-surgeon in the world, the
winner of the Ironman competition, Jack the Ripper, and every
astronaut who ever went into space. You have twenty-four hours a
day to use, invest, or waste. Time is the great equalizer. It knows
no racial, cultural, socio-economic, or age boundaries. God gives
you the gift of time and makes you trustee of your allotment.

Pulitzer Prize winner Annie Dillard wrote, "What then shall I
do this morning? How we spend our days is, of course, how we spend
our lives. What we do with this hour, and that one, is what we are
doing. A schedule defends from chaos and whim. It is a net for catch-
ing days. It is a scaffolding on which a worker can stand and labor
with both hands at sections of time. A schedule is a mock-up of reason and order—willed, faked, and so brought into being; it is a peace
and a haven set into the wreck of time; it is a lifeboat on which you
find yourself, decades later still living. Each day is the same, so you
remember the series afterward as a blurred and powerful pattern."[1]

How will you use your days? What will be the pattern of your
life? Time is limited. There are only twenty-four hours in a day.
Within that limitation you must do what you will do. Time will not
expand. It comes down to making choices—this over that.

RELATIONSHIPS ARE BUILT ON CHOICES

Early in our marriage, my husband made two decisions that strengthened our relationship. First, he put our date night on the calendar. The very act of committing himself in black and white communicated to me that our relationship was important to him. He jotted my name in one square every week to ensure that "we" didn't get lost in the midst of all the events, projects, and people boiling around us. Prior to this decision, it seemed that often *something* would come up to preempt our time alone.

Second, Roger determined he would consider our date night of highest importance. It did not surprise me when our first scheduled date was threatened by a phone call. A young man wanted to come over to discuss a problem he was having. After assessing his situation on the phone, Roger told him, "I have an appointment tonight. Come for breakfast in the morning." Roger's decision declared more profoundly than words ever could that our relationship was important to him. A date with me was as inviolable as an appointment with a pastor, senator, or doctor.

Our choices say a lot about us, about what is important to us. Too often our choices betray us when they reveal what we hold dearest. They are the truest gauge of our values.

Mary's Great Choice

How would you like to have Jesus give you two thumbs up and tell you, "Good choice!"? What kinds of choices get an enthusiastic response from the Lord? Look at Jesus' commendation of His friend Mary:

> As Jesus and his disciples were on their way, he came to
> a village where a woman named Martha opened her
> home to him. She had a sister called Mary, who sat at the
> Lord's feet listening to what he said. But Martha was dis-
> tracted by all the preparations that had to be made. She
> came to him and asked, "Lord, don't you care that my
> sister has left me to do the work by myself? Tell her to
> help me!"

"Martha, Martha," the Lord answered, "you are worried and upset about many things, but only one thing is
needed. Mary has chosen what is better, and it will not
be taken away from her." (Luke 10:38-42)

Jesus was a guest in Martha's home. While Martha was busy
with all the practical preparations, her sister Mary sat at Jesus' feet
listening to Him. When Martha complained to Jesus that she was
doing all the work while Mary was sitting, Jesus replied, "Only one
thing is needed. Mary has chosen what is better, and it will not be
taken from her."

Jesus commended Mary for her choice—to take time to give
Him her attention. What was that best choice? A Greek word picture for "what is better" is the idea of the "best dish on the table."
Jesus uses the imagery of a long buffet table festooned with choices:
smoked salmon to apple cobbler and everything in between. Jesus
says that when Mary chose to sit at His feet, she was choosing the
best dish. Why did He use a food image? I think He wants us to
realize that although we have many options, a relationship with
Him is the one dish that meets our deepest needs. Only friendship
with Him nourishes the soul.

For Mary, for Martha, and for us, there are always other things
we could do instead of developing our friendship with our Lord.
Good things. Profitable things. Helpful things. There are always
other appealing "dishes." But Jesus said, "Only one thing is
needed"—only one thing is absolutely necessary.

What is that "one thing needed"? Relationship with Him.

What is that "best dish on the table"? Relationship with Him.

What does Jesus commend? The *choice* to cultivate a relationship with Him. Time to listen. Time to speak. Time to unite hearts,
minds, and wills. Nothing is more important in His eyes.

One Choice Leads to Another

The choice to cultivate our relationship with the Lord requires that
we make other choices as well. Emilie Griffin writes, "Spiritual formation involves a fundamental choice. Choosing to live for Jesus
Christ may mean adopting a certain style of life, or, perhaps more

properly, a rule of life. We take on a series of spiritual practices that will open us to God's work in our lives."[2]

Quiet time is a practice that you choose to make a part of your day because relationship with God is a high value. When Griffin uses the term "rule of life," rule does not mean *rules* as in a legalistic "do list." A rule is a thoughtful, deliberate decision to live a certain way. The decision—like the decision Roger made to write my name on the calendar or Mary's decision to sit at Jesus' feet—establishes the value as a practice. The resolve is made and then reaffirmed every day.

Someone might ask, "Why do I have to have set times to meet with God? Isn't it better just to come to God when I really feel like it? Isn't that more sincere?" The truth is that we have more control over our *actions* than over our *feelings*. Make your feelings submit to your choices, not the other way around. Feelings often follow in the wake of firm decision. Established patterns keep us from crashing during spiritually low periods.

For some people, choices are straightforward, cut and dried. For example, Scott has committed to meet with God every morning and floss his teeth every night. Period. Those decisions are made. But for Scott and the rest of us, the choice to meet with God every morning opens the door to a host of other choices.

- What time do I need to go to bed if I'm getting up at 5:30 to have a quiet time?
- Do I need to forego the late night news in order to get up on time?
- Will I shower and eat before or after quiet time?
- Will I wait until after quiet time to pick up the newspaper or turn on the radio or TV?

These secondary choices serve our decision to spend time with God. They enable us to live out our highest values. In the seemingly insignificant multitude of smaller choices lies the success or failure of our goal.

ESTABLISHING BOUNDARIES

Boundaries are the choices you make once you've determined to keep space in your life for God. We imitate God's pattern when we set boundaries to keep everyday life from crowding out our time with the Lord. God ordained boundaries for our well-being and protection. He said, "Six days you shall labor and do all your work, but the seventh day is a Sabbath to the LORD your God" (Exodus 20:9-10). Just as the ocean glorifies God when it stays within the boundaries set for it, we glorify God when we set limits that allow us to seek God first (see Matthew 6:33).

Of course, the idea of seeking God first is not primarily about sequence. The idea is not to have a quiet time first thing in the morning, check it off your to-do list, and get on with the rest of life. *Seeking first* is the focus of a lifetime, all day, in every circumstance. Quiet time is a practice you develop because you want God to be foremost in your life all day long. You consecrate a block of time solely to the Lord, to give Him your undivided attention as you start each day. You lay the first stone of an altar in the morning—alone, in quiet—and then throughout the day stack stone upon stone as you worship God in your work, play, and dealings with people.

Kudzu, Machetes, and Making Space for God

Kudzu, an extraordinarily fast-growing plant, was imported from Japan to stem erosion problems in the southern part of the United States. It's been described as ivy on steroids. The charging vines spread like a lava flow, covering everything, even climbing trees and pulling them down. Kudzu galloped across the South, beautifully green, and smothered whatever it could.

I once read about a man who laid aside his lunch box and picked up his machete each day when he came home from work. Before he kissed his wife or kicked the shoes off his weary feet, he did battle with the kudzu, which grew a foot a day at the edge of his property.

The pressures and opportunities of your life are like kudzu. Unless you continually hack them back within set boundaries, they will creep and climb into every crevice, pulling down your spiritual life. Like a tidal wave of kudzu, the concerns of life can engulf you—

your thoughts, your time, your energy—leaving nothing for cultivating a friendship with God.

Like preparing a hole for a new tree or marking a date night
on a calendar, quiet time is making space to grow in your relationship with God. Acknowledge that the kudzu of your life will
crowd out time with God unless you are vigilant. Take up the
machete. Resist the crush and press of lesser things. Set boundaries.
Choose again and again to seek God first. Come to your quiet time
each new day to affirm that you will make and protect a space in
your life for God.

I keep a glass candy jar filled with rice and five walnuts. If I
dump out the walnuts and rice and pour the rice into the jar first,
the walnuts will not fit. But if I put the walnuts in first, the rice
sifts in around the nuts and the lid easily seals atop. This visual prop
reminds me that I must manage my time to ensure that what's
important doesn't get lost amid the less significant things of life. If
I do the everyday things of life (work, shopping, laundry, errands)
first, I probably won't find space to fit in quiet time. But if I make
time with God a priority and do it first, the rest of life seems to shake
itself in too. Setting priorities means determining what comes first
in order of importance.

GROWING A RELATIONSHIP

You may be asking, "Exactly what do you mean by a 'relationship with
God'?" This question is an important one. Relationships are difficult
to define even among humans. How much more difficult to define
a relationship between the Creator—the invisible, holy, infinite
God—and a human being. If you're going to make the choice to set
this relationship as a priority, you'll want to understand it.

Personal and Unique

I see my husband sitting in his chair morning after morning, year
after year, meeting with the Lord. I gaze at his face as he prays and
think how much I would like to be able to slip into what he is experiencing with the Lord. But that's impossible. I can experience my
own relationship with the Lord and I can experience the Lord *with*

my husband, but I cannot experience *his* relationship with the Lord. Like a marriage, the exclusive number is two. Just as no two marriages are alike, no two relationships with God are alike. Relationships are shaped by our individuality.

My relationships with our three children, whom I love dearly and equally, are unique. They each bring their distinct personalities to our relationship. All relationships are expressions of the people involved, their affections, tensions, styles, values, and so on.

In the previous chapters we considered the *how* of quiet time. "How" can be discussed only in very limited terms, however, because quiet time is a vehicle for cultivating a relationship, not an end in itself. Like other relationships, our relationship with God is one of a kind. A relationship is a mysterious thing. It cannot be dissected and examined. To scrutinize it with the intent of codifying, evaluating, and defining it is to kill it. And no relationship is more mysterious than the believer's union with Christ.

The Bible teaches that I am "in Christ" and that He is "in me" (see John 14:20). This image He uses to help me understand our relationship is profoundly intimate. Something organic has taken place. Jesus and I are attached like branches and vine of the same plant (see John 15:5). Jesus says that His followers are His body (see Ephesians 5:30). My life in Christ is something alive and is always changing, either growing or withering. Jesus desires to express *His* life absolutely and uniquely in and through *me*. Quiet time is a regular, scheduled meeting with God to allow *His* mind, *His* will, *His* love, and *His* power to find fuller expression in my life (see John 14:10-12).

His Purpose, Your Purpose

It was God's purpose, His plan, to die for you to make you His beloved forever. God intends that your salvation (in the fullness of what that means) and your friendship with Him be *your* purpose. Clear aims keep your life on course and channel your energy toward the goal. A noble and well-defined direction gives shape and order to your days. A controlling purpose helps you hone in on your relationship with God. Set your eye on the one thing needed and move forward.

RELATIONSHIPS NEED TIME, COMMUNICATION, AND LOVE

Your purpose is clear. Your boundaries are set. What's next? You can look forward to meeting with the God who loves you and desires your friendship, day after day, for a lifetime. As you come to your quiet time with the Lord, remember that every relationship needs cultivation. Just as a farmer tills the soil and fertilizes it for a fruitful harvest, you too must engage yourself if a friendship is to grow. Three essential elements are needed: time, communication, and love.

Time

A. W. Tozer wrote about the importance of spending time with God:

> It is well that we accept the hard truth now: the man who would know God must give time to Him. He must count no time wasted which is spent in the cultivation of His acquaintance.[3]

We've already talked about the limitations of time. If you are going to meet with the living God, who is your life, time must be taken from something else.

Communication

Our God is a communicating God. He gave us a Book that reveals His innermost thoughts. He has given us His Spirit to live in us and to communicate with our spirits (see John 14:16-17,26). He urges us to talk with Him about everything (see 1 Thessalonians 5:17). Heart-to-heart talks are so important to God that He records in the Bible many of His conversations with individuals.

Alfred Barrett wrote:

> Incense is prayer
> That drives no bargain.
> Child, learn from incense
> How best to pray.[4]

The Bible speaks of our prayers as a sweet incense rising to God: "May my prayer be set before you like incense" (Psalm 141:2).

"Another angel, who had a golden censer, came and stood at the altar. He was given much incense to offer, with the prayers of all the saints, on the golden altar before the throne. The smoke of the incense, together with the prayers of the saints, went up before God from the angel's hand" (Revelation 8:3-4).

This image speaks of God's great delight in our communication with Him. Our prayers may seem halting and bungling to us, but they waft up to God as sweet and fragrant incense. As we come before God, willing to be shaped by His will, our words and thoughts ascend as a holy offering to Him.

Communication with God "drives no bargain." My friend Lee said he learned this from the "weaned child" mentioned in Psalm 131:2. The challenge to him was that while a nursing child comes to his mother in a functional way, a weaned child comes close just for the pleasure of her company. Communication with God is not reciting a monologue or presenting Him with your "shopping list." Real communication involves a sympathetic receptivity to attune your heart to God. Draw near like a weaned child and let the incense rise.

Love

Marriage counselors tell us that we can knock ourselves out trying to express love to another person and miss completely. Each person has his or her own language of love. For some it might be a gift, for another a love letter, for another physical or verbal expressions of affection. In the same way, if we want to communicate love to God, we need to know His language of love. Fortunately, we don't have to blunder about by trial and error. God has told us what speaks of love to Him. The primary means is obedience. He says, "If anyone loves me, he will obey my teaching. My Father will love him, and we will come to him and make our home with him" (John 14:23). We demonstrate our love by taking God seriously when He speaks, and then conforming our lives to His revealed will. Praise and thanksgiving are expressions of love only if obedience accompanies them.

Cultivating your relationship with God will take some effort on your part. Work at keeping space in your life for God. Your life will be the richer for it.

⬛SUMMARY⬛
Our choices, primary and secondary, enable us to make and preserve space in our lives for God. Relationship with God is the "best dish" among all the possibilities of life. It falls to us to hack back the busyness of life and choose to make room for Him.

⬛MAKING IT PERSONAL⬛
- Continue following the quiet time plan you have chosen.
- Identify any changes you need to make to hack back the kudzu, to put the walnuts in first, to let your prayers rise like incense. What is one specific application you might make this week?

⬛REFLECTION AND DISCUSSION QUESTIONS⬛
1. Describe the kudzu of your life. What choices will help you create and preserve a space for God in your life?

2. Besides quiet time, what might be another walnut in your jar? What ideas do you have for making the "rice of life" sift in around them?

3. Did any of the ideas in this chapter cause you to think differently about your communication with God? In what way?

4. Your relationship with God is unique, organic, and dynamic. How is your friendship with God growing and changing?

5. Your obedience expresses love to God. Is there any step of obedience you believe He wants you to take?

6. Share with the group or a friend a thought from your quiet time.

FIVE

Victory over Obstacles, Secrets to Consistency

SALLY SAYS SHE'S TRIED MEETING WITH GOD EACH DAY BUT HAS never succeeded in pulling it off more than three days in a row. After failing to be consistent yet again, she feels guilty, defeated, and discouraged. Can she ever hope to meet with God on a regular basis?

Randy leaves for work in the wee hours of the morning. He wants to meet with God but is stymied by his schedule. His wife, Carol, cares for their three young children and rarely gets to sit. When she does, she usually falls asleep. Are there solutions for their dilemmas?

STRUGGLES? JOIN THE CLUB

Anyone who makes quiet time a consistent part of life's journey will find obstacles in the path. But by putting into practice a few ideas that have helped others meet regularly with the Lord, you can face these challenges with steadily increasing success. This chapter also will give you some practical tips for more meaningful reflection, or meditation, in your quiet time.

Obstacles come in many forms. Some are exterior (time pressures, circumstances), others are interior (blockages of the heart, mind, and will). Perhaps you pray, or try to, but the time seems forced or distracted. Or maybe you read the Bible but come away more confused than blessed. Perhaps your mind wanders or you feel groggy when you read or pray. Whatever shape your obstacle takes, you are not alone.

Joseph Cardinal Bernardin, the late archbishop of Chicago, wrote, "Lord, I know that I spend a certain amount of that morning hour of prayer daydreaming, problem-solving, and I'm not sure that I can cut that out. I'll try, but the important thing is, I'm not going to give that time to anybody else. So even though it may not unite me with you as much as it should, nobody else is going to get that time."[1]

To reserve time just for God has value in itself. An appointment with God, faithfully though imperfectly observed, speaks of our intention and desire to know and love Him.

Like Cardinal Bernardin, we each bring our flawed humanity to our time with God. But we also bring the Holy Spirit, who lives inside us, to translate and transform our experience (see Romans 8:26-27). The presence of both our human frailty and the powerful Holy Spirit creates a tension between *expecting too much* and *being satisfied with too little*.

Think of your relationship with God as a plant affected by a multitude of forces: climate, soil conditions, temperature, moisture, sunshine, disease. In Luke 8, Jesus tells a parable about a farmer who sows his seed (God's Word) into a variety of soils. Jesus says the soil of some lives is hard, compacted like a well-trod path. Nothing penetrates that ground. Others gladly hear the Word, but the soil of their lives is like shallow pockets of dirt sifted on rock with no place for roots to take hold. The plants living in this soil wither under scorching sun and gusting wind. The third soil Jesus mentions is soft enough and deep enough, but it is infested with weeds. Thorns encircle the tender plants, soak up precious nutrients, and choke out life, preventing health and maturity. The weeds God mentions surprise me: life's worries, riches, and pleasures. At first glance they seem innocuous. Respectable, even. But these "weeds" and others like them keep us from connecting with God the way we want to.

OBSTACLES WE FACE

Worries

The first "Word-choking weed" that Jesus mentions is life's worries. Everyday life can strangle the Word of God. Nothing big, perhaps, just the normal demands, concerns, and pressures we all face. Merely living can consume all our physical, mental, and emotional energy and asphyxiate tender spiritual sprouts.

Like most passions, worry grows as we feed it—and it is always hungry. Worry refuses to sit quietly in the corner; it demands our attention and energy. Our worries often grow out of what *might* happen but what probably *won't* happen. We needlessly expend emotional energy on remote possibilities over which we have no control. Worry is useless; it changes nothing (see Matthew 6:27).

Don't let worry steal your attention away from God. Believe that God is good and that He will be good to you. He knows the future. He cares about you and is powerful enough to meet your needs.

My friend Diane says, "Worry, fear, and anger are like Satan throwing sand in your eyes. It distracts you from doing the one thing that will make a difference: believing God."

When worries drain away your spiritual vitality, list them in your quiet time notebook. Pray over each situation, applying the truth of Proverbs 3:5-6 or James 1:5. As you pray over your worries one by one, ask God if there is any action He wants you to take. Record any prompting He gives you and then act on it. If God brings no specific action to your mind, hand the worry over to Him. Your quiet times can be rich and meaningful if your worries lead you to take hold of God's Word and to offer prayers of faith.

Riches

Geri had to give strict attention to every penny. Then she unexpectedly came into a large inheritance. She thought her worries were over. Instead, she found that managing this windfall ate up more of her time and energy than pinching pennies did. While money is not bad in itself, it can draw our hearts and eyes away from the Lord. C. S. Lewis wrote:

One of the dangers of having a lot of money is that you
may be quite satisfied with the kinds of happiness
money can give and so fail to realise your need for God.
If everything seems to come simply by signing checks,
you may forget that you are at every moment totally
dependent on God.[2]

Either dearth or abundance (and everything in between) can
avert our attention from focused devotion to Christ. It is impossible
to serve both God and money (see Matthew 6:24).

Pleasures

As with riches, pleasures can divide our loyalties and divert our
attention away from God. The pleasures may be innocent in
themselves, but they become dangerous when they are in competition with God. John Henry Jowett feared "the restless
scattering of energies over a multiplicity of interests," which left
no margin of strength or time for "receptive and absorbing communion with God."[3]

My friend Julie refers to this as "the pleasure pull." She feels
acutely the tension created for a disciple of Jesus Christ in a world
packed with interesting things to do and places to go. Like Jowett,
she fears spreading herself thin in a pleasurable but shallow
existence.

Busyness

In his book, *Tyranny of the Urgent*, Charles E. Hummel wrote, "Your
greatest danger is letting the urgent things crowd out the important."[4] A frantic life is not conducive to the life of the Spirit. Quiet
time is not intended to be one more pressure in an already over-
loaded life. Except for those special situations—a new baby, natural
disasters, sickness, and the like—if you are too busy to spend consistent time with God, you are too busy. Nothing curbs busyness
more effectively than determining to live by what is truly important. Structure your days around quiet time and your life will gain
a new simplicity.

Lacking a Sense of Awe

Hasidic Jews always precede the reading of the Scriptures with the phrase, "And God spoke." According to tradition, whenever Rabbi Zusya heard that preliminary phrase, his emotions would overcome him. The other rabbis would have to lead him away as he ranted, pounded the walls, and incessantly cried, "And God spoke." Rabbi Zusya never heard the words spoken by the Lord. It was enough to unhinge him in awe and wonder that God spoke to humankind.

Every phrase of Scripture should send us ranting too, if only we could cut through our personal fog. If we had any idea at all who God is, every phrase would flatten us. It must confound the angels of heaven that we are bored by the prospect of hearing God speak to us. If we had our spiritual wits about us, who could get any further than "Jesus loves me this I know, for the Bible tells me so"? As the psalmist writes: "Let all the earth fear the LORD; let all the people of the world revere him" (Psalm 33:8).

Tell God you're sorry for being insensitive to His glory. Ask for an increased sense of who He is and who we are as created beings. Ask for a growing sense of awe. Keep coming to Him. He knows your weak humanity. He loves you and is trying to break through to you all the time.

Procrastination or Laziness

Many of us put things off — important things, critical things. We let our days ooze away in lesser pursuits and never quite get around to giving God our attention. The book of Proverbs is instructive and challenging for anyone struggling in this area. Proverbs teaches that blessings follow those who *diligently* pursue wisdom and that calamity besets those who don't. If you're struggling with procrastination or laziness, get a boost by having quiet times in Proverbs this month.

Fatigue, Depression, or Grief

When Diane returned to the United States after many stressful years overseas, she experienced the extreme weariness that accompanies prolonged major adjustments. Her personal reserves were depleted as she served her family's needs. During this time, Diane copied ten handwritten pages of Bible verses on faith into her notebook. In her quiet times she focused her attention on these verses. "I directed my mind to believing God, not toward problems or discouragement," she explained.

To help you when these times come, start now by writing in your notebook verses that stir you to greater faith. When you need extra encouragement to trust God, that section of your notebook will be a valuable resource.

Little Spiritual Appetite or Desire

Our son Graham determined to fast for a week before leaving the state for a new job. He often sat with us at the table even though he was not eating. After several days, I asked him if it was getting harder. On the contrary, he said he experienced little hunger. Neglecting food for a brief time can actually diminish hunger. Could you be lacking an appetite for time with God because you have not been "eating" regularly? Spiritual appetite, like physical appetite, is stimulated by good food, regular exercise, and invigorating company. If your hunger for God and His Word is at low tide, these ideas may get you back into deeper water. Start with a small, but tasty morsel.

STIMULATING SPIRITUAL APPETITE

Have your quiet time in Philippians 4:6-7 every day this week. Each day:

- Copy the verse in your notebook.
- List your current concerns.
- Pray about your concerns one by one. Ask God to work on your behalf.
- Thank God that He hears. Thank Him that He wants to use each of these situations to draw you to Himself in deeper trust and to give you a history of experiences with Him.

(See Appendix for additional appetizers.)

Crazy Schedules and Peculiar Situations

Jim has his quiet time before he leaves the house for work at 4:45 A.M. He gets up at 4:00. In the past, he has gotten up as early as 2:30. With this kind of schedule, why is he so committed to a morning quiet time? Jim tried lunch time, but interruptions hindered his consistency. Evenings didn't work either; he fell asleep. Fortunately, he wakes up fairly quickly (his wife, Sharon, needs two cups of coffee to get her eyes open), so he decided early mornings are a good time for him. Jim spends fifteen minutes reading the Bible and writing his thoughts and insights in a fat, four-by-six spiral-bound notebook. He continues his meditation and prays as he makes the round trip from Denver to Casper, Wyoming, in his UPS tractor-trailer rig.

If your schedule is unusual, you may have to experiment as Jim did to find the best time. Don't give up! Keep working at it. The challenge can be met with creativity — and perhaps, if necessary, sacrifice.

Legalism, Guilt, People Pleasing, and Performance Syndrome

"I had a flat tire this morning. I knew something would happen because I missed my quiet time." This earnest young woman misjudged God. He is not looking down from heaven with a clipboard in His lap, handing out gold stars if we have a quiet time and flat tires if we don't. Misconceptions about God can put us into performance mode. We make checklists for ourselves. A perfect record obligates God to bless us; a few blank spaces on the chart defeat us and cause us to withdraw from God. But that's not how it works — God does not love us more because we have a quiet time.

Susan said her quiet times were performance-oriented. She came to Christ in college and was part of a campus fellowship. Group members often shared something from their quiet times and asked Susan how her time alone with God was going. She met with God nearly every day as self-protection against their inquiry.

Warren, also a new believer, was part of the same group. Whereas Susan cringed when others shared from their time alone with the Lord, Warren leaned forward with relish, hungry to learn all he could. Years later, when Susan evaluated the fellowship group's impact on her, she felt it led her into people-pleasing performance. But Warren considered it a gift and a privilege to be in a spirited group that encouraged its members to seek God individually and corporately.

The writer of Proverbs said, "Above all else, guard your heart, for it is the wellspring of life" (Proverbs 4:23). It is the heart that matters. Susan knew she *should* have a quiet time; Warren *wanted* to have time with God. Susan had a quiet time to please people; Warren met with God and was grateful that people helped support this new practice.

Are you meeting with God or with a habit? With God or a duty? With God or a command? Because you want to or to win the approval of others? If your heart is right, habit helps, duty is delight, command is not burdensome, and even imperfect fellow believers are a source of joy. To the imperfect heart everything becomes a hindrance, but to the perfect heart everything serves the purposes of God. Thomas Boston, the Scottish mystic, wrote, "When the soul is heavenly, it will even scrape jewels out of a dunghill."[5]

Wandering Mind or Sleepiness

Jay walks as he prays. He paces the room and prays out loud. He says that if he kneels or sits, he succumbs to drowsiness. He also says that he gets his exercise as he talks to God. Physical movement helps him keep his mind centered on God. Like Jay, learn what helps you stay engaged and alert during your quiet time.

Here are ideas that will help you enter into your quiet time more completely:

- Pray aloud or write out your prayers.
- Rather than fight a wandering mind, make the ideas that persistently intrude bow before Jesus. Here's what I mean. When a phone call you need to make or a problem you face threatens to divert your attention from God, bring it before the Lord. Make a note in your notebook and pray about it. Offer it to God: "Lord, grant me wisdom regarding this call. I want to glorify You. Please lead me in the words and spirit of the conversation."

- If you are coming to your time with the Lord fresh from the hubbub of getting children off for school or if you're racing to get yourself off on time, it helps to build a bridge from the hectic world to the place of quiet with God. Here's a suggestion: Read briefly from a book that has ministered to you in the past to help you refocus your attention, warm your heart, and bring you before God with a more pliable and surrendered spirit. The idea is not to get through the book, but to read just enough to slow down, change gears, and center your thoughts on God. Or you may want to create a section in your notebook of favorite verses, hymns, poems, and quotes to span the gap into more meaningful time with God.

Disappointment in Your Prayer Time

Scott is a businessman who meets with the Lord in his family room with windows overlooking Puget Sound. One morning Scott complained, "Lord, I'm disappointed in my prayer time. I'm making an effort, but . . ."

"Really? You're making an effort?" Scott heard the Lord's rebuke. "Look at you lounging back in your easy chair, coffee in hand, feet up. Who do you think you're talking to? Get on your knees." Since then, Scott gets on his knees to pray.

Pray about your prayer time. You may be surprised what God might say to you.

Unholy Thoughts

Before coming to Christ, Ron used pornography. After his conversion, vile images from the past sometimes invaded his mind when he prayed. This caused him great distress, but he found several things that helped:

- He thanked God that he has been delivered from that life through Jesus Christ.
- Next, he shared his background and continuing problem with a trusted Christian friend and asked for prayer. When Ron openly shared his past addiction and exposed

it to the light, he experienced immediate release from the shame and bondage. Sins kept in secret crouch in dark corners, waiting to ambush us. Shine God's light on them.

■ Ron continued to foster purity of mind and heart through regular quiet times with the Lord. He rejected impure thoughts and cultivated a taste for what is true, noble, pure, lovely, admirable, excellent, and praiseworthy (see Philippians 4:8).

If you are battling an addiction or are plagued by some sin that persistently defeats you, try implementing the three steps that helped set Ron free.

Unrealistic Expectations

Kathy attended a conservative Bible college and was taught that quiet time was twenty minutes of Bible reading, twenty minutes of prayer, twenty minutes of Bible study. Then she found herself knee-deep in toddlers—and defeated. What was possible and appropriate for her as a student was impossible for her as a mother. Could God be happy with anything less than an hour? Of course. God is tenderly aware of your situation and sympathetic to it. "He tends his flock like a shepherd: He gathers the lambs in his arms and carries them close to his heart; he gently leads those that have young" (Isaiah 40:11).

TIME AND TIME AGAIN: SECRETS OF CONSISTENCY

We've explored some of the obstacles that threaten our daily time with the Lord and have considered possible ways to surmount them. Now we're going to shift slightly to look at principles that promote consistent quiet times.

According to the dictionary, *consistency* deals with agreement of parts, harmony, regularity of action. The word comes from the root "to stand firmly." A lifetime of meeting with God is exactly the kind of practice that is "in harmony" with our claim to love Him. One would expect those who profess to be disciples of Jesus Christ to make room for Him in their lives every day.

Alan grew up in West Virginia observing his father's consistent practice of devotion. With assurance Alan said, "I can tell you what my eighty-five-year-old father did this morning. He got up at 5:30 and read his Bible and prayed." What a legacy to leave a son—the unshakable confidence that Dad met with God this morning as he has every day for years on end.

Here are a few tips to help you be more consistent in quiet time:

Remember Why

Clarify again in your own mind why you believe it is worth the effort to carve out time alone with God. If your reasons aren't clear, you won't be able to sustain the practice. Your decision to meet with the Lord must become something organic that takes root in your heart and mind. The most motivating reality is that God wants *you*. He wants your heart, your mind, your soul, and your strength (see Deuteronomy 6:5). Nothing is more pleasing to Him than receiving your love and trust. God wants you to fix your eyes on Him all day long, but I believe He most enjoys the daily time you set aside to focus entirely on Him.

Recognize and Respond

Acknowledge that any desire you have to meet with the Lord is the Holy Spirit's gracious work in you. Respond to it. And if you come to quiet time with little desire, thank God for what little you *do* have and ask Him to increase it.

Don't Let the Fear of "Legalism" Derail You

Some might argue that it's legalistic to meet with the Lord every day just because you know you should. But because you know *why* it is important to have a quiet time, it's not legalistic to spend time with God—even on days you don't feel like it. Living life can't be reserved for times of inspiration and enthusiasm. The world would be in chaos if all of us didn't operate to some extent out of "habit" and "shoulds" based on predetermined values.

Keep Plodding

As with most things in life, success comes to those who move steadily in the direction of their goal. "The sluggard craves and gets nothing, but the desires of the diligent are fully satisfied" (Proverbs 13:4). Be diligent to meet with God.

Exercise Discipline
If you are going to *get up in time* to have a quiet time in the morning you must *go to bed on time* at night. Both decisions require discipline.

Follow a Plan
No one who meets with the Lord haphazardly, who opens his or her Bible randomly and reads here or there before snapping the Bible shut, continues long or with much satisfaction. A plan gives continuity, making each day another link in an ongoing history with God.

Engage and Enrich
The more fully you involve yourself in your time with God, the more likely you will consistently keep your date with Him. One of the best ways to do this is to learn how to meditate on God's Word.

ENRICHING QUIET TIME THROUGH MEDITATION
Jesus calls us to feed on His life. "Just as the living Father sent me and I live because of the Father, so the one who feeds on me will live because of me" (John 6:57). But how do we *feed* on Jesus?

Let me give a physical example of this spiritual principle. In our family, everyone had to eat a little of the vegetable served at dinner. When our son Matt was a child, he detested lima beans. He took the three beans on his plate and swallowed them whole like pills.

Unfortunately, we often read the Bible in the same way. We gulp it down without tasting it. Instead, we need to chew the words, roll them around in our mouths, and suck the sweetness from them. This process is called meditation. Meditation comes from the idea to "revolve in the mind" or to "ruminate." Rumination brings to mind a cow, a ruminant, chewing its cud. The cow eats, swallows, and then later regurgitates and rechews in an ongoing cycle.

The Lord calls us to a life of meditation and promises tremendous benefit to the "chewer." "Do not let this Book of the Law depart from your mouth; meditate on it day and night, so that you may be careful to do everything written in it. Then you will be prosperous and successful" (Joshua 1:8).

Christian meditation differs greatly from meditation taught by eastern religions. They tell their practitioners to empty their minds; God tells us to fill our minds with His truth. Eastern meditation is passive; God wants thinking brains, involved emotions, and deliberately yielded wills.

As an art history student, I learned something about meditation from an assignment. I was to write a two-thousand-word paper on a vase housed at the Baltimore Museum of Art. No research allowed, only observation. I remember circling the vase, wondering how I could possibly say so much about this one object. But the more I looked, the more I saw. I scribbled notes about its shape, color, texture, materials. I wrote about the design painted on it, the story that scene might depict, how the vase might have been used in the past, how I would use it if it belonged to me. This is a process very much like Christian meditation.

PRACTICAL MEDITATION EXERCISES

1. In the Middle Ages, readers were encouraged to read aloud, to taste the words, to listen to "the voices of the pages." Try this. Choose a verse and read it over and over, each time emphasizing a different word. Try Psalm 46:10, for example: "**Be** still and know that I am God . . ." "Be **still** and know that I am God . . ." "Be still **and** know that I am God . . ." Continue through the verse. Linger on each word, tasting and savoring. You will be amazed at the punch even a seemingly insignificant word like "and" can have on your life.

2. Henry Ward Beecher carried precious stones in his pocket. At odd moments he would extract one, hold it to the light and enjoy the radiance. Meditating on God's Word is similarly holding the truth before your eyes and giving God the chance to shine His light on it, that you might enjoy it and make it more fully your own. God's Word belongs to every believer equally, but every believer doesn't possess it equally. Ask questions as you think about the Bible. What does it say about God? About you as a human being? About you as a believer in Jesus Christ? Are there any instructions to follow? Any promises to claim? Any attitudes to adjust? Any warnings to take to heart?

CHOOSE LIFE

As young men in the Army years ago, my husband, Roger, and a friend were seeking together to follow God. His friend confessed that his time alone with the Lord was inconsistent. Roger probed, "Did you have breakfast this morning?" "Yes." "Did you have breakfast yesterday?" "Yes." "Did you have breakfast every morning this week?" "Yes." The question might be adjusted: Did you read the newspaper? Make a telephone call? Watch a television show? Play a computer game? Go out with friends? You see the point. We make time for what we really want to do or what we are convinced is important. God thinks our relationship with Him is of greatest importance. He speaks of it in terms of life and death:

> *"This day I call heaven and earth as witnesses against you that I have set before you life and death, blessings and curses. Now choose life, so that you and your children may live and that you may love the LORD your God, listen to his voice, and hold fast to him. For the LORD is your life. . . ."*
> (Deuteronomy 30:19-20)

And in Deuteronomy 32:47: "They are not just idle words for you — they are your life. By them you will live long in the land you are crossing the Jordan to possess."

God and His words are *your life*. God charges you to "choose life" and "choose blessing." Shape your life around the decision to spend time alone with your Lord. Choose to give His Word prominence in your day. Your choices define your days, your years, your life. Your choices will either lead you into real life or into death. Choose to make time with God a consistent part of daily life.

■SUMMARY■

All believers face obstacles as they seek to meet with God. Keep working at making this time with God central to your life. Engage yourself more fully through meditation. Choose life.

▓MAKING IT PERSONAL▓

Enrich your time with God by incorporating a meditation exercise in your quiet time. (Refer to the ideas on page 79.) Try one of these ideas in your quiet time this week.

▓REFLECTION AND DISCUSSION QUESTIONS▓

1. Describe the exterior (your circumstances) and the interior (your heart, mind, will) hindrances to rich, daily time with God that you currently face.

2. Read Exodus 16. What similarities do you see between quiet time and God's instructions for gathering manna?

3. John Knox (1514–1572) wrote, "Let no day slip by without your receiving some comfort from the mouth of God. Open your ears, and He will speak pleasant things to your heart."[6] What "comfort" or "pleasant things" are you receiving from your time with the Lord?

4. In Psalm 119:95 the writer puts together two unexpected ideas: "The wicked are waiting to destroy me, but I will ponder your statutes." In what ways do you think meditation on God's Word might help in this situation?

5. In light of Psalm 119:95, write a similar statement that reflects something you are facing: "Office politics swirl around me, but I will meditate on God's Word" or "My infant is not sleeping through the night, but I will meditate on God's Word." Do the benefits that you listed in question 3 apply to your circumstance? In what ways?

6. For you, what is the secret of consistency in quiet time?

SIX

The Write Stuff

EACH CHAPTER OF THIS BOOK HAS SUGGESTED THAT YOU write during your quiet time. Why? Because reading and writing are biblical ideas. Our God chose to reveal Himself and His plans most fully in the Book He wrote for us. The Bible contains sixty-six books written over two thousand years, all to communicate to us His mind, heart, values, and purposes. God elevates the written Word forever because He is a writing God.

Repeatedly, God commands that things be written down. We know that He has a book of life with every believer's name written in it (see Philippians 4:3). There are other books in heaven, as well (see Revelation 20:12). God Himself inscribed the Ten Commandments on the tablets (see Exodus 32:15-16). God instructed His people, "Now write down for yourselves this song and teach it to the Israelites and have them sing it" (Deuteronomy 31:19). God even had the conversations of those who fear Him recorded (see Malachi 3:16).

Do you wonder why writing is so important to God? Surely it's not because He needs an aid to His memory. The benefit must be for us. Perhaps in heaven God will have scrolls, which record our prayers or our conversations with one another, read aloud that we might all praise Him for His great faithfulness to us during our years on earth. Whatever His reasons, He has modeled for us the importance of putting what is of spiritual value into black and white.

WHY WRITE IN YOUR QUIET TIME?

There is value in writing in your quiet time even if it is merely to copy a verse out in your own hand or to type it into your computer. The Lord gave this instruction for kings in Israel:

> *When he takes the throne of his kingdom, he is to write for himself on a scroll a copy of this law, taken from that of the priests, who are Levites. It is to be with him, and he is to read it all the days of his life so that he may learn to revere the LORD his God and follow carefully all the words of this law and these decrees and not consider himself better than his brothers and turn from the law to the right or to the left. Then he and his descendants will reign a long time over his kingdom in Israel.* (Deuteronomy 17:18-20)

I read this and wondered if it really meant that the king should make the copy with his own hand, or was he simply to assign the task to someone else? Surely a king had plenty of important state business to attend to. Wouldn't it be wiser to delegate that task to a scribe? I called a Hebrew scholar with the question. The answer? The king was to make his own copy, the personal, time-consuming way—by hand, letter by letter. God intended that the king model for the nation esteem for and submission to His Word. He was to keep his handwritten copy within reach and to read from it all his days. We don't know for sure that any king made his own copy, but I suspect David did, based on Psalm 119.

When you write, even if you are just copying the text in front of you, you engage another sense—the tactile. Writing makes demands on an additional part of your brain. Your total person is more fully involved. Writing slows you down and keeps you from bounding over ideas without really touching on them. When you take the time to write something down, you make it more fully your own. The act of writing brands the thought with your mark, but more important, the thought is given the opportunity to mark you.

You don't have to be a "writer" to benefit from pen and paper in your quiet time. Even doodles, diagrams, lists, and sentence fragments can help you process more deeply and think more critically about the ideas God is giving to you.

Writing Promotes Meditation

If merely copying text has benefits, how much more does writing that emanates from a more thoughtful engagement with God's Word. Henri Nouwen explained, "Writing can be a true spiritual discipline. Writing can help us to concentrate, to get in touch with the deeper stirrings of our hearts, to clarify our minds, to process confusing emotions, to reflect on our experiences, to give artistic expression to what we are living, and to store significant events in our memories."[1]

Thoughts can remain deceptively foggy until you are pressed to choose precise words to accurately communicate them. Copy a portion of Scripture and then jot down your questions, observations, ponderings, and conclusions. Specific and intensely personal applications often emerge as you see ideas take form in black and white. Ancient Chinese wisdom says that recreating something in words is like being alive twice.

Writing As an Aid to Memory

Repeatedly, God tells His people to remember. Unfortunately, it seems that throughout the ages we have excelled in forgetting—especially the things that are most important in life.

Most of us know the value of a written "do list," an address book, or notes taken in classes or business meetings to help us remember. Scott, a businessman, says taking notes is like taking photos on a trip. It gives you something to come back to, to remember, to enjoy again. The same benefit applies to our times with the Lord. We become better stewards of what God shows us in our quiet times if we capture something on paper for future reference. The exercise demonstrates our intention to take the encounter with God seriously, to reflect on God's words and to grapple with their meaning and application.

For example, when Israel decided that the tall guy hiding among the baggage was their choice for king (see 1 Samuel 10:22-25), the prophet Samuel wisely sought to bring some sense to the process. "Samuel explained to the people the regulations of the kingship. He wrote them down on a scroll and deposited them before the LORD" (1 Samuel 10:25). This scroll served as a reminder of what God intended and expected. It was also a symbolic and tangible reaffirmation of God's covenant with His people.

Like Samuel, copy parts of the Bible that speak to your current situation. If you are facing a major decision, you might write out verses that speak of God's presence and guidance (see Deuteronomy 31:6, Psalm 16:8, Psalm 32:8, Proverbs 3:5-6, Isaiah 41:10).

Pen As Teller

Whenever the light goes on in your understanding, God is giving you a gift. Spiritual truth comes by spiritual means and should not be taken for granted. Unfortunately, even what is of great significance fades away in time. Taking notes will help you hang on to what God gives you. Quiet times preserved in writing may be returned to again and again.

Over the years, I periodically have pulled down a past quiet time notebook to see what God was speaking to me about three months or three years ago. Often I have felt a pang of regret as I read. God had met with me, had given some insight or instruction, and although I had received it with gratitude at the time, I treated it lightly, passing on to new revelations without a backward glance.

As I read these past quiet time pages, I find that the insights, which had stirred me three months or three years ago, still flame up when I return to them. They are words to me from God. These revelations are gifts to be attended, considered again, run through the grid of my current circumstance, prayed over, and applied afresh. Themes and threads surface. For example, as I revisit my quiet time notebook, I may see a pattern of sin that escaped notice before. Instead of becoming aware of a specific sin only as it pops its head above the surface now and then, I see it liberally scattered throughout my life. The impact of accumulation gets my attention. This sin is not an occasional failing, but a well-rooted weed. This kind of periodic review and reflection helps me to identify needs, to confess sin, and to turn again to God for His work in this area of my life.

It's funny but true that writing helps us know what we think. Novelist E. M. Forster wrote, "How do I know what I think until I see what I say?"[2] We start to write, and unfolding before us on the page is evidence of what we know and an awakening to what we don't know. Pen and paper reveal to us what we think, what we know and don't know.

WHAT TO WRITE?

Diagrams, Charts, Sketches

We all have different learning styles, and many of us are visually oriented. A picture, diagram, chart, or cartoon helps us see a truth more clearly. If you are this kind of learner, include sketches or scratch down your thoughts in pictorial form.

PICTURING THOUGHTS

When I was studying Psalm 3, I drew a box and labeled the sides Pray, Rest, Work, and Trust to help keep the truth before me visually.

Verse 4: "To the LORD I cry aloud, and he answers me from his holy hill." (Pray)
Verse 5: "I lie down and sleep." (Rest)
Verse 5: "I wake again, because the LORD sustains me." (Work)
Verse 6: "I will not fear . . ." (Trust)

"Snowballing"

Just as a baseball-sized snowball gathers layer upon layer as it rolls, an insight from your quiet time can grow over a period of time, if you are alert. Making notes will help you keep the channels open and your antennae up for anything that might enrich your understanding of a topic. For example, as you read your Bible, you may be troubled by a question about the content or you may have an interesting thought about the passage. You scribble the question or thought in your notebook. Perhaps tomorrow you will gain further insight from your reading. On Sunday, your pastor may add a layer to the subject. A radio preacher, a song, a comment by a friend—they all may add thought upon thought. You go on shamelessly pilfering until your baseball-sized thought is as big as a snowman.

Writing not only helps us build insight upon insight, but it increases the probability that something from our "snowball" will spill over to others. As our note taking brings greater clarity and order to our own minds, we carry away a small portable package that might enrich someone else. Author Jill Briscoe keeps a stack of postcards and her address book nearby and prays, "Who needs this thought as much as I do at this time?" She says that often a name pops up and she dashes off a postcard, including a thought from her devotions.

Paper, Pen, and Prayer Requests

From time to time I find a piece of paper that strengthens my faith—an old prayer list, yellowed with time. Whenever one of these treasures falls out of an old notebook or a Bible no longer seeing daily service, I am astounded. Prayers, long forgotten, have been answered. My heart rises in praise to God and I make a renewed commitment to pray, knowing that God hears my prayer and in some mysterious way is moved by it.

Because each day has troubles of its own, I express today's concerns to God. Unfortunately, I tend to forget the circumstances that severely exercised my heart only days before. The pattern is natural: I am occupied with today's problems; yesterday's concerns are of no consequence. I move through life focused on the immediate circumstances and fail to look back. The answered prayers of the past are largely lost to me. Even if I set aside time to reflect on what God has done, I find it difficult to remember past prayers. The situation is further complicated by the fact that God often answers in unexpected ways so that I don't recognize the answers when they come.

Referring back to previous requests refreshes my memory and enables me to perceive the work of God in answer to prayer. This bulks up my faith muscle so that I come to my current circumstance with a fresh heart to trust God. A written prayer list facilitates remembering, stimulates faith, and preserves a record for future generations.

At one time, Yori used a bookkeeping ledger to record requests and answers. Currently she uses a four-by-six, spiral-bound notebook, which she keeps in her purse or by the phone. When someone asks her to pray for something or a need occurs to her, she jots down the request before she forgets. She uses colored highlighters to distinguish categories: family, others, events, and so on. When a request is answered, she strikes a line through it. At a glance, she can run through family requests or see answered items for praise.

My husband uses index cards secured with a rubberband (what would we do without rubberbands?) to help him move through his prayer time in an orderly way. He writes out promises from the Bible that have special significance for him to pray over. He also has a series of cards containing the names of those he prays for daily. With each name he has written specific things he will pray for that person. After he goes through his daily cards, he begins circulating through another series of cards that includes a wider circle of people he wants to pray for regularly. In the past he has used different color cards for his daily requests to easily separate them from the others. As prayers are answered, he jots down the date and how the request was answered.

Writing Prayers

Because Phyllis sometimes has her quiet time in a restaurant, she finds that writing out her prayers keeps her from distraction and gives a record of what she has talked to God about.

Augustine (354–430 A.D.) penned a series of eloquent, soul-searching prayers entitled *Confessions,* which have influenced the church for centuries. In these prayers, Augustine reviews his life in God's presence and lays bare his heart before God.

Like Augustine, you might want to review your life consciously and deliberately in written prayers. Recall your early days in Christ. Consider the gracious way God brought you to Himself, how He made you aware of your need for salvation. Record milestones in your life: answers to prayer, the sense of gratitude you felt when you first heard Christmas carols and understood the meaning of those wonderful words, the kindness of God to you in the tough times you have weathered.

Consider copying prayers from the Bible (see Ephesians 1:17-19, 3:16-19, Philippians 1:9-11, Colossians 1:9-12, 2 Thessalonians 1:11-12, Philemon 4-7). Use these prayers as templates. Personalize Paul's prayers by inserting the names of those for whom you pray. For example, you might pray: "Glorious Father, please give Matt the Spirit of wisdom and revelation so that he might know You better. Enlighten the eyes of his heart in order that he might know the hope to which You have called him, the riches of Your glorious inheritance" (based on Ephesians 1:18).

JOURNALING YOUR JOURNEY

Throughout the ages, people have used journals to help them think more perceptively about their lives. Some have used their journals as a diary to record the events of their lives, their travels, or their work. Fortunately, many followers of Christ have kept a journal to record their spiritual journey. These journals were valuable to them and now are valuable to us. We read over other people's shoulders and benefit from their struggles and their wisdom.

John Wesley diligently kept journals—twenty-six bound volumes—in which he recorded his vision and ideas, missionary activity, answers to prayer, personal insights from the Bible, and the great workings of God in his midst. Here is an excerpt dated December 23–25, 1744:

> While I was reading prayers at Snowsfields, I found such
> light and strength as I never remember to have had
> before. I saw every thought, as well as action or word,
> just as it was rising in my heart; and whether it was
> right before God, or tainted with pride and selfishness. I
> never knew before what it was "to be still before God."[3]

The *New York Times* ran an article on the value of journaling, citing Dr. James W. Pennebaker's findings. His studies indicate that journaling has benefits for our physical and mental well-being. Writing about traumatic experiences was even found to raise the level of T-cells that fight infection and virus. How does that work? As long as our problems are undefined, our thought process often resembles a dog chasing his tail. We go round in circles, getting ever more heated but coming no nearer to resolution. Getting things down in black and white helps us think more objectively about them. It helps us organize our thoughts and see errors in our thinking.

For followers of Jesus Christ, journaling must move beyond "letting it all hang out" on paper. While that may have therapeutic value on one level, God desires that we gain a deeper connection with Him—that our minds become transformed by His truth and our actions become shaped by His purposes. So as we read our thoughts spilling out on paper before us, the Holy Spirit often seems to read over our shoulder and bring the overlay of biblical truth. He makes comments to us: "I know that's how you feel, but it isn't true." (Then He often brings a Bible verse to mind.) "Adjust your thinking." (Then He might encourage and direct.) "Operate by faith." "Trust Me." "Show love." "Remember I am committed to you." "Fear not." "Take heart." The process of journaling moves us from natural human thinking to truth, from chaos to order.

Barb was well-established in the practice of quiet time when she hit an emotional wall. When her last two daughters left home, she stood numbly staring at their empty closets. She came to her morning time with the Lord unable to concentrate. During this time Barb found it helpful to untangle confusing emotions by writing about them. As her thoughts and emotions took shape on paper, they eventually formed a bridge back into quiet time as she knew it before.

Roger begins each day's quiet time by reviewing the previous day. He sits with his yellow pad resting on his lap and writes. He records events and seeks to understand the significance of them. As he thinks about yesterday, he might note an action to take or an attitude to confess and address. His observations lead to prayer, to notations on his "do list," and to reading in the Bible. This daily reflection keeps his devotions anchored in real life. Yesterday's lessons are applied to life today. His journal helps him live a more fully integrated life, a life where his quiet time is relevant in everything he does.

A SAMPLE JOURNAL ENTRY

Your quiet time notebook is a wonderful place to capture thoughts from God. Here is a section from my journal written during a half-day alone with the Lord:

April 28, 1998
Hebrews 4:14-16: "Therefore, since we have a great high priest who has gone through the heavens, Jesus the Son of God, let us hold firmly to the faith we profess. For we do not have a high priest who is unable to sympathize with our weaknesses, but we have one who has been tempted in every way, just as we are—yet without sin. Let us then approach the throne of grace with confidence, so that we may receive mercy and find grace to help us in our time of need."

My thoughts: My weakness is not my problem; my "strength" is! Jesus is able to sympathize with my weaknesses; He was tempted just like I am. I am called to come boldly into His presence by virtue:
- *of His being tempted and being sympathetic,*
- *of His sinlessness,*
- *of His effective sacrifice,*
- *of His freely offered mercy and grace.*

Sweet Jesus, ascended Son of God, I come before You.

Again weakness is my route to blessing. In Matthew 5:3-10, the Lord promises blessing to those who are poor in spirit, mourners, meek, hungry, thirsty, and persecuted.

2 Corinthians 12:9-10: "But he said to me, 'My grace is sufficient for you, for my power is made perfect in weakness.' Therefore I will boast all the more gladly about my weaknesses, so that Christ's power may rest on me. That is why, for Christ's sake, I delight in weaknesses, in insults, in hardships, in persecutions, in difficulties. For when I am weak, then I am strong."

My thoughts: Part of my problem, my sin, is that I like to be strong, able, adequate—not weak and needy. The root of pride is SELF-adequacy, SELF-confidence, SELF-love, SELF-interest, SELF-protection.

Psalm 32:9: "Do not be like the horse or the mule, which have no understanding but must be controlled by bit and bridle or they will not come to you."

My thoughts: If I have understanding I will recognize my need for God and come to Him without being pressured by outside forces. This is why quiet time is so important—to remind me that I am needy, that my need puts me where God can show His strength.

Throughout the ages, believers have used pen and paper (or their equivalent) to record something of their personal history with God. The Psalms, for example, are songs or poetry that document and preserve for us David's intimate experience with God—his insights, petitions, praises, failures, questions, struggles, and hope. We can know the same benefits of writing today.

Read the Word and pray. Ponder. Then go one step further: Capture in writing something of the content and the spirit of what you are learning, thinking, praying, or questioning. Try writing out your prayers or making notes on what you read. Experiment. Discover which ideas fit you best at this time in your life. With pen in hand, allow God to take you beneath the surface into a deeper experience with Him.

▪▪SUMMARY▪▪

Writing is a biblical idea. Practice writing something down in your time with the Lord. It will help you stay engaged and make you a better steward of what God says to you. Bring order and freshness to your prayer time by putting your pen to work.

▪▪MAKING IT PERSONAL▪▪

Whether you decide to mark your Bible, journal your journey, write out your prayers, or try some other idea from this chapter, employ your pen in your quiet time. Take a moment to specify what you will apply from this chapter this week:

Remember, you don't need to change anything you are doing or add anything if you are consistently meeting with the Lord and your spiritual appetite is being satisfied.

▓▓REFLECTION AND DISCUSSION QUESTIONS▓▓

1. What reasons for writing in your quiet time seem most significant for you?

2. What idea from this chapter did you incorporate into your time with God this week?

3. How has writing in your quiet time notebook enhanced your relationship with the Lord so far?

4. What problems have you encountered in making writing part of your quiet time?

5. Consider setting aside a quiet time to read over some past entries in your notebook. What do you see that reminds, encourages, or challenges you?

6. How do these verses enrich your thinking about the importance of writing in your quiet time: Deuteronomy 6:9; 10:2; 17:18-20; 27:2-3,6-8?

SEVEN

Doing Time: Persevering in Dry Times

A FEW YEARS AGO, I ACCOMPANIED MY HUSBAND TO THE EAST Coast for a surgery. I knew no one in the town we were in and stayed alone in a hotel near the medical center. Much of each day I sat by Roger's bed, and every evening I returned to the hotel room. Ordinarily I love large blocks of time alone, but this room echoed the hollowness I felt inside. Several days into our time there, I found myself unable to make simple decisions. I wandered in weaving paths around the hospital cafeteria just trying to choose something for lunch. Every morning and every evening I met with the Lord, but I had little sense of connecting with Him.

The surgeon had predicted a seven-day hospital stay. Although the surgery went well, medical complications prevented Roger's release after a week. Two or three days more, the doctor thought. Weary and discouraged, I returned to the hotel room for a nap. The housekeeper's sharp rap on the door startled me. I was even more startled when she asked me how soon I would be out of the room. We had reserved the room only for seven days — my reservation was expired. The hotel was fully booked. My inner works were shaking and threatening to blow apart. Where was God's grace and peace?

For all the world it looked like God had run off with the grace and peace, leaving me (a quivering mass of emotional jelly) to face "homelessness" in a crime-ridden city. God's peace and grace were gifts I was used to and, I suppose, took for granted. Now, in my extreme weakness, I glimpsed what I would feel like *all the time* apart from His compassionate and indulgent care. Under these circumstances, I faced my poverty and absolute need for Him to work. I knew God had not deserted me, but I had no evidence of His presence. I read His living Word and it was wooden to me. I prayed and my prayers wedged in my throat. But even in the worst of it, I knew that He was near, standing just out of sight, in the shadows. I knew, too, that He was sustaining me, but not comfortably nor triumphantly. The rest of the story is one of God working everything out in ways that spoke unmistakably of His hovering, warm presence. As Puritan John Flavel wrote, "Thy God may turn away His face, He will not pluck away His arm."[1]

All believers face times when God seems distant, when our hearts seem insensitive to spiritual realities. In the extreme, these times have been called "the dark night of the soul." The Puritans called these barren times "God desertions." Their theology wasn't flawed. They knew, just as we do, that God has said, "Never will I leave you; never will I forsake you" (Hebrews 13:5). But they also knew that, at times, God can and does withdraw the *sense* of His presence, leaving us dry, lonely, and empty. In 1832, Robert Murray M'Cheyne expressed it succinctly in his journal, "Mind unfitted for devotion. Prayerless prayer."[2]

On April 11, 1772, Francis Asbury penned: "Found inattention to study, an unsettled frame of mind, much insensibility of soul, and a backwardness to prayer. Lord, help me with an active warmth to move, and with a vigorous soul to rise!"[3]

DRY, BUT NOT COOL

What is spiritual dryness? Where does it come from? Why does dryness inflict even those who love and serve God?

It's important to distinguish between spiritual *dryness* and spiritual *coolness*. They aren't the same thing. In dry times, we miss the *sense* of God's presence. The Word may be lifeless and prayer mechanical. We desire the intimacy of former days, but it eludes us. Spiritual coolness, on the other hand, results when we cling to the sin God points out to us and refuse to turn from it. A chilled spirit lacks an appetite for the things of God and is accompanied by hardness and resistance.

Of course, there is always sin in our lives. Even in the most devout, there are sins committed, virtues omitted. None of us knows the heart and holiness of God completely. None of us loves the Lord perfectly with all our heart, soul, mind, and strength (see Deuteronomy 6:5). None of us flawlessly loves our neighbors as ourselves (see Luke 10:27).

It can be difficult to distinguish between spiritual dryness and spiritual coolness. When you're not sure which you're experiencing, it's good to inquire of the Lord, "Lord, is there any sin I am cherishing (see Psalm 66:18) or refusing to acknowledge (see Psalm 32:3-5)? Is there willful disobedience and resistance to Your will and Spirit?" If God reveals sin in you, confess it and turn from it. Repentance is a way of life for the follower of Christ. It is agreeing with God about your sin and changing your mind and your ways to conform to His will. As you learn what God wants from you, make adjustments. "Repent, then, and turn to God, so that your sins may be wiped out, that times of refreshing may come from the Lord" (Acts 3:19).

But what about spiritual dryness? The Bible gives us examples of how some men of faith experienced dryness. Quiet time was not always great for David, the psalm writer. You don't have to read very far in the Psalms to see that, spiritual giant though he was, David knew dry times too. Times when God seemed absent, remote, and uninvolved. Psalm 13 is a good example.

How long, O Lord? Will you forget me forever? How long will you hide your face from me? How long must I wrestle with my thoughts and every day have sorrow in my heart? . . . But I trust in your unfailing love; my heart rejoices in your salvation. I will sing to the Lord, for he has been good to me. (Psalm 13:1-2,5-6)

David was "dry," but not "cool." Even though he did not experience the intimate nearness of God, he continued to voice his questions to Him. The distance David felt between himself and God did not keep him from pouring out his deepest feelings to God and asking for His help. David did not enjoy the sweet fellowship he usually knew, but he made his requests with tender confidence, and he trusted God's unfailing love.

Job expressed a similar sense of God's absence in the midst of troubles. We know that Job's trials came upon him *because he was righteous*, not because he was wayward. Even in his agony, Job trusted God. Even though God seemed unreachable, Job, like David, knew that God was involved and working out His purposes (see Job 23:3-12).

If even deep and godly people can lack a sense of God's presence, how should we think about these times when they come? Richard Foster, in *Celebration of Discipline*, wrote:

> What is involved in entering the dark night of the soul?
> It may be a sense of dryness, depression, even lostness.
> It strips us of overdependence on the emotional life.
> The notion, often heard today, that such experiences
> can be avoided and that we should live in peace and
> comfort, joy and celebration, only betrays the fact that
> much contemporary experience is surface slush. The
> dark night is one of the ways God brings to us a hush, a
> stillness, so that He may work an inner transformation
> upon the soul.[4]

A spiritually dry time doesn't necessarily indicate an unhealthy soul. Unpleasant as dry times can be, we need only read the journals of great men of God like Francis Asbury, John Wesley, David Brainerd, or a host of others to know that dry periods come to all—and that they are beneficial if we respond properly.

WHY DRY TIMES COME

If sin is not the cause—if even spiritual giants experience dry times—how should we think about these parched periods? Why do they come?

To Seek Him

Sometimes God withdraws the sense of His nearness to see if we will seek Him. Sometimes He withdraws to increase our hunger for Him. When we are deprived of His company, we rethink our relationship with Him. Just as shapes stand out more clearly in winter as we see the sharp, distinct forms of trees without leaves, the dry, desert landscape may help us see the essential shape of life in Christ in new ways.

To Remember His Grace

Dry times remind us that our relationship with God is a gift, given by His grace. We do not obtain, sustain, or maintain it ourselves. Spiritual vitality is not something we ensure by having morning devotions, doing Bible study, or sharing our faith. Spiritually barren times work a kind of brutality on our pride. In the desert we confront our desperation for God to work in us. "Unless the LORD builds the house, they labor in vain" (Psalm 127:1-2).

The oasis we so desire may actually be more dangerous than the desert if we think we deserve or have earned the lush place where we stand. God responds always to the humble and contrite person who trembles at His Word (see Isaiah 66:2). Humility means *depressed in mind or circumstances, afflicted, lowly, needy, poor.* Contrite, as used in Isaiah 66:2, means *smitten, lame, maimed, dejected.* Not our usual picture of the victorious Christian. But God runs to the aid of the weak and needy one who looks to Him for help. God says His strength is displayed most perfectly in our weakness (see 2 Corinthians 12:9).

Humility and contrition do not diminish us as people—they make us authentic. They allow us to face our fallenness and more fully appropriate the mercy and grace of God.

Physical Conditions

Some dry periods have a physical cause. We are complex in our interrelations between our physical, spiritual, chemical, and emotional parts. A new medication, fatigue, hormonal imbalance, or a host of other factors may also affect our times with the Lord. "Spiritual problems" may actually be medical in nature. See your physician if you suspect this to be the case.

LIVING BY FAITH IN DRY TIMES

Dry periods are part of God's training program for you, giving you an opportunity to rely more fully on Him. "Who among you fears the LORD and obeys the word of his servant? Let him who walks in the dark, who has no light, trust in the name of the LORD and rely on his God" (Isaiah 50:10). This is addressed to one who fears and obeys God and yet experiences darkness—who perhaps lacks a sense of God's presence or a clear direction.

Dryness, like the rest of life, must be faced with faith, by faith. God is the one who transforms the desert soul. When we ask, "Can God spread a table in the desert?" the answer, of course, is a resounding, "Yes!" In Psalm 78:19-31, the writer details God's kind and abundant provision for His people in their desert wanderings.

When you go through dark or dry times, persevere with the Lord. Believe He is near though your senses tell you otherwise. Believe His promises. Trust His character. God doesn't discard. He reassures, repairs, revives, and refreshes. (For a list of other "re-" words to meditate on in your quiet time, see Appendix, page 138).

Don't lose heart if you are experiencing spiritually dry times. God still walks beside you. He still hears your prayers. He uses dryness to see if you will walk by faith, not sight (see 2 Corinthians 5:7), by faith, not feelings. This will lead you nearer to His heart. Come to God grateful for what He chooses to give you, even if it's continued dryness.

Paul, an editor friend, says that when dry periods come after months and years of regular meetings with the Lord, there is a stability and peace even in the dryness. The pattern of consistent quiet time weaves a fabric of truth and reality that sustains us in the drought. No matter how long the desert trek, humbly keep your quiet time with Him, even if you feel you're the only one showing up for the date.

SPIRITUAL LUSHNESS: KEEPING HOT

Although every believer faces times of spiritual dryness, this condition is not normative. God calls His children to be "fervent in spirit" (Romans 12:11). One translator phrased it "boiling over."

In the spiritual realm, an elevated temperature is one sign of health. God wants us to be hot spiritually. The Bible gives us instruction for keeping hot.

Make an Effort

Sometimes we confuse living under the Spirit's control with lack of effort. God never intended that we glide along on a spiritual high. Make every effort to engage yourself with God. Peter wrote, "For this very reason, make every effort to add to your faith goodness; and to goodness, knowledge; and to knowledge, self-control; and to self-control, perseverance; and to perseverance, godliness; and to godliness, brotherly kindness; and to brotherly kindness, love. For if you possess these qualities in increasing measure, they will keep you from being ineffective and unproductive in your knowledge of our Lord Jesus Christ" (2 Peter 1:5-8).

Tend the Fire

God instructs the priests, "The fire on the altar must be kept burning; it must not go out. Every morning the priest is to add firewood and arrange the burnt offering on the fire and burn the fat of the fellowship offerings on it. The fire must be kept burning on the altar continuously; it must not go out" (Leviticus 6:12-13). Hold this picture in your mind as you come to your quiet time. Like the priests, daily add fresh fuel to the fire in your soul. Take up the sacred Word of God and kiss the pages with your heart and will. Gather your heart, mind, strength, and soul deliberately in God's presence and commune with Him. Day after day, offer yourself as a living sacrifice on the altar (see Romans 12:1) and fan the flame by adjusting your attitudes and actions in willing obedience. Commissioner Brengle of the Salvation Army somewhere said, "Keep the draught open; clear the ashes out; keep putting in fuel."

Grow in Knowledge

Two dejected disciples trod the road from Jerusalem after the crucifixion and resurrection (see Luke 24:13-35). They rode an emotional rollercoaster in these last days, and they were rattling down to the bottom distressed and confused. They thought that Jesus was the Messiah, but crucifixion shattered that hope. Then some of the women claimed that they had seen Jesus risen from the dead.

When Jesus fell in step with these two disciples, they were kept from recognizing Him. As they walked, Jesus began to explain, using the entire body of Scripture, that it was the plan of God for the Messiah to suffer, to die, and to rise from the dead. Later, when they realized that Jesus had been with them, they said, "Were not our hearts burning within us while he talked with us on the road and opened the Scriptures to us?" (Luke 24:32).

Time in the Lord's presence and a growing knowledge of God and His plans produces burning hearts. New insights strike sparks in a life. A fresh perspective on "how all the Bible fits together" becomes a stack of kindling that ignites a bonfire. Are you growing in your information and your understanding of the things of God?

Be a "One-Thing" Person

The challenge never to be lacking in zeal, but to keep your spiritual fervor (see Romans 12:11), might be linked to Psalm 27:4: "One thing I ask of the LORD, this is what I seek: that I may dwell in the house of the LORD all the days of my life, to gaze upon the beauty of the LORD and to seek him in his temple." Zeal is a fire in the heart. Passion cannot be spread broadly to encompass everything. Passion is a channeled river, not a pervasive swamp. People of "one thing" are the hot ones. Are you too scattered to be hot?

Return to Your First Love

The Lord gives this advice to a church that had cooled in spiritual fervor: "Remember the height from which you have fallen! Repent and do the things you did at first" (Revelation 2:5). Jesus said they had lost their "first love," or "bride love." The Lord described it this way: "I remember the devotion of your youth, how as a bride you loved me and followed me through the desert, through a land not sown" (Jeremiah 2:2).

When was your love for God freshest and deepest and sweetest? Recapture and relive those times in your mind. Has the bride in you, who considered no hardship too great a price for the pleasure of being by your Lover's side, given way to a self-centered, self-protective, grouchy, and tetchy "old wife"? Did you once sing hymns to Him spontaneously? Did you take walks conscious of God's presence? Did you step out in daring acts of obedience? Did you have a quiet time in the morning and again before you went to bed? Do it again. Consider the height from which you have fallen and turn again toward Him in love and self-abandoning devotion.

Delight Yourself in the Lord

Delight is a cultivated affection. Delight presupposes focused attention, a pause to enjoy, to relish God. Is life so busy that you rush past everything and delight in nothing? Slow down. Ask God to give you that same delight Job expressed: "I have treasured the words of his mouth more than my daily bread" (Job 23:12). Rev. J. C. Macauley said:

> Teach my heart, set free from human forms, the holy art of reading thee in every line, in precept, prophecy, and sign, till all my vision filled with thee, thy likeness shall reflect in me. Not knowledge but thyself my joy! For this I pray.[5]

Remember How Much You Have Been Forgiven

Jesus gives us another clue to maintaining a great love for Him. A woman with a sordid past washed Jesus' feet with her tears, dried them with her hair, then kissed his feet and poured perfume on them. His host on this occasion, however, did not greet Jesus with a kiss or provide water for him to wash His feet (all customary courtesies at this time). Jesus attributed the discrepancy in their behavior to two things. One, the woman knew she was a sinner, while His host, a Pharisee, thought of himself as a good man. Two, she experienced the joy of release from guilt because her *many* sins were forgiven. The Pharisee, on the other hand, never faced his sinfulness and, therefore, never received cleansing. Jesus sums it up this way: "Therefore, I tell you, her many sins have been forgiven—for she loved much. But he who has been forgiven little loves little" (Luke 7:47).

A dry period is a great time to recall again how much you have been forgiven (see Psalm 103:12, Isaiah 43:25). Whether the problem is a cool heart or a dry spirit, no better elixir exists than to linger at the foot of the cross. The gospel is a fountain of life, a stream of refreshment, a surging ocean bringing wave after wave to wash over the parched soul. That God became man and moved among His creation to seek and save the lost is a cool cloth on a fevered brow. That God died in your place, for your sins, voluntarily, gladly, to bridge the chasm between Himself and you is a cup of cold water to a desert wanderer and a bellows blast to dying coals.

Revisit Old Altars

Jacob flees from Esau and spends the night camping out with a stone for a pillow (see Genesis 28:10-22). There God meets with Jacob and personalizes promises made to Abraham years before. The next morning Jacob uses his "pillow" as the first stone in an altar he erects to God. Jacob calls the place "Bethel," house of God, and makes a vow to God. Later in Jacob's life, God calls Jacob to return to Bethel (see Genesis 35).

What altars can you return to? Think of your conversion experience as an altar to revisit. Recall the times God met with you in meaningful ways and pilgrimage to that time in your heart. Specific physical locations or objects may evoke memories of a special connecting with God. For example, my husband says the road where I lived when he was courting me triggers strong stirrings of gratitude to the Lord for giving us to each other. Another road where God spoke words of encouragement and promise to him as he walked and prayed is a holy place to him. Recently we returned to that road to pray about a major decision we were facing.

Get Physical

Like the road we returned to, the tangible world can serve our spiritual journey. A smooth rock inscribed with a date, a subject, a place, and two Scripture references (and sealed with clear fingernail polish) resides on my desk. This fairly nondescript stone represents an answer to prayer, a very personal miracle, and reminds me that nothing is too small for His kind attention.

Be alert to ways that the material world can enhance your fellowship with Jesus Christ. The Bible is full of physical images that can assist you in grasping spiritual truth. For example, the apostle Paul speaks of putting on the whole armor of God in Ephesians 6:10-18. My friends Buck and Molly "put on their armor" each morning, often before they get out of bed. They do this by praying together through this passage, "buckling on the belt of truth," and so on. The strong imagery of this passage helps them visualize in a vivid way what is happening on the invisible spiritual level.

For a specific exercise to help you think more deeply on the Cross, see the Appendix of this book for a "Stations of the Cross" exercise I developed (page 136). Our Lord's death and resurrection are the pivotal events in the history of humankind. But somehow, through familiarity, we tend to sanitize and neutralize the accounts recorded at the close of each gospel. This contemplation of the events surrounding the death and resurrection of Jesus Christ puts you in the action.

Gratitude

"Give thanks in all circumstances, for this is God's will for you in Christ Jesus" (1 Thessalonians 5:18). Thanksgiving is the key element in the prayer of faith that brings peace (see Philippians 4:6-7) and opens spiritual doors into God's presence. A thankful spirit readies the heart to receive from God or to content itself in seeking Him.

George MacDonald wrote, "For what people are accustomed to, they regard as coming from nobody; as if help and progress and joy and love were the natural crop of Chaos or old Night."[6]

Do you take for granted the sunrise, your breakfast, the ability to see the faces of those you love? Ingratitude hardens the heart. You cannot always be by the ocean or on a mountain top, but you can cultivate alertness to glories close at hand: the wood grain in a tabletop, the color and texture of a piece of fabric, the sound of water dripping off bushes at spring thaw. These small wonders can jostle you out of a dazed existence so that you remember again how much God cares for you. Then, your gaze settles on the Cross; you wonder at His love for you. In this way, gratitude softens and warms your heart.

When More Is More

Sometimes a little bit more makes a huge difference—say, five minutes more. Add five minutes to the beginning of your quiet time to sing hymns. Or add five minutes at the end to sit quietly and listen or to capture some insight in writing. Or elongate your time of reflection. An extra five minutes invested in the most important things of life pays great dividends.

When Less Is More

Some people are spiritual gluttons. They attend multiple Bible studies, continuously listen to radio preachers, and poke their proverbial finger in every spiritual pie, from Christian concert to prayer meeting. They mistakenly think that a rich diet will produce spiritual vitality.

Unfortunately, overeating produces sluggishness. Spiritual food must be *digested* as well as *ingested*. We deaden our spiritual life when we gulp down knowledge without meditation and application. Mistaking "knowing" for "being" is the first soul-blunting step toward hypocrisy.

Music, Music, Music

Is music ever a part of your date with God? Do you sing? Put on a tape? Music is an important part of worship—private and corporate. The Psalms are 150 songs, prayers, and journal entries all rolled into one. The Lord commanded Moses to write down the words of a song (see Deuteronomy 31:19). The words of some old hymns carry the weight of inspiration. Music sets a mood and often fosters a freer expression of emotion. I often start my quiet time singing: "Holy, holy, holy; Lord God Almighty, early in the morning, my song shall rise to Thee."

Obedience Stokes the Fires of Faith

The Bible makes clear that God wants to make His home in the human heart. Jesus said, "If anyone loves me, he will obey my teaching. My Father will love him, and we will come to him and make our home with him" (John 14:23). Quiet time helps you make your life a more hospitable place for God if it leads you to obey. Apply personally the commands and warnings of Scripture. Instead of being stuck in a rut, you will find yourself energized by His love.

BREAKING OUT OF YOUR RUT

- Come into the Lord's presence as you might come into your boss's office to get instructions for the day.
- Get a red-letter edition of the Bible (where the words of Jesus are written in red) and read only His words.
- Look for a specific idea as you read, like the *hope we have in Christ* or *how Jesus handled unbelief in those he met* or *the love of God.*
- Vary your location. Have your time with God at a coffeeshop on the way to work or on the porch swing or in a different room. If you usually sit, kneel. Put on music for part of the time. Devote an entire quiet time to listening quietly before the Lord.
- Include a devotional book (see suggestions on page 144).
- Do you find yourself praying the same things over and over again? Note the great prayers of Scripture (see 1 Chronicles 29:10-19, Daniel 9, Matthew 6:9-13, Colossians 1:9-14). Use them as a guide for your prayers. Pray what the apostle Paul prayed, or pray through the passage you are currently reading. In this way, let God determine the topic of your conversation with Him.

Bounce Out of Ruts

The police thought they discerned a pattern to a recent string of bank robberies and predicted that on a particular day a certain bank would be robbed. The police hid in a dumpster at the site and popped out when the robbers arrived. Proof positive that ruts can be dangerous to your health.

Occasionally I consider dying my hair flaming red, becoming a nun, or blowing the budgeted grocery money on horseback riding lessons. Every life needs a little shaking up from time to time. Every relationship profits from a gentle jarring of the status quo. The same is true in our relationship with God. Not that I introduce some new element to get His attention afresh; the need is mine. Even in something as unthinkably thrilling as meeting personally with God, my human tendency drifts toward lethargy, toward presumption, toward deadening, mindless ruts.

Chrysostom said, "A table with only one sort of food produces satiety, while variety provokes the appetite."[7]

I thrive on both consistency and variety. Established patterns, like meeting daily with the Lord, foster stability and growth. Variety, within that stability, provides stimulation. Spiritual disciplines are essential to maturity in Christ, but spiritual ruts are numbing. George MacDonald wrote, "Nothing is so deadening to the divine as an habitual dealing with the outsides of holy things."[8] Habits are not deadening, but habits practiced indifferently are.

Rethink your quiet time. Have you veered off course? Gotten bogged down? Lost sight of Christ, your true goal? Remember, Bible reading is not an activity, an assignment, a discipline, or drill, but a means of opening lines of communication with God. Prayer isn't a grooved recitation, but a stream from the heart.

---

10 QUESTIONS TO ASK IF YOUR SPIRITUAL LIFE IS DULL AND DRY

1. Are you confessing and turning away from your sin?
2. Are you meeting with God regularly?
3. Are you engaged in practices that dull your spiritual sensitivity?
4. What were the conditions around your best times with the Lord?
5. Have you fallen into a rut?
6. Is poor health or fatigue a factor?
7. Are you praying for God's blessing on your life (1 Chronicles 4:9-10) and enlisting others to pray for you?
8. Have you asked God what He is seeking to teach you through this time?
9. What is one practice or attitude that might breathe fresh air into your times with God?
10. Have you told the Lord that you will come to your quiet time even if the dry times continue?

▪▪SUMMARY▪▪

Dry times serve the purposes of God in our lives. But the model of the Christian life is one of "fervency of spirit," of "boiling over." Trust and seek God in dry times and do what you can to stoke the fires.

::MAKING IT PERSONAL::

Pray over the ideas in this chapter. Ask God: "Is there any action I need to take? Any attitude I need to adjust? Any prayer I need to pray?"

::REFLECTION AND DISCUSSION QUESTIONS::

1. What is the difference between *spiritual dryness* and *spiritual thirst*? Is there a connection?

2. Dry times come to everyone. When you face dry times, what attitudes and responses will best serve the work of God in your life?

3. What has been your experience with spiritual dryness or spiritual coolness? What helped you regain "heat"?

4. How do you respond to this quote by Georges Bernanos: "Vice is less dangerous to the soul than staleness or mediocrity"?[9]

5. What ideas from previous chapters have you included in your quiet time? Which ideas would you recommend to others? Why?

6. How might you implement some suggestion from this chapter in your quiet time this week?

EIGHT
Longer Times with God

TIME IS A MEDIUM OF EXCHANGE. WE EXCHANGE OUR TIME FOR something: money, success, food, sleep, leisure, a clean house, or a shiny car. To give time to one thing requires that we take time from something else. Life is full of choices. We can't add an hour to our days or escape all the demands of life, but we can exercise choice.

TIME AND THE WILL OF GOD

The Bible calls us to live wisely, understanding what the Lord's will is in regard to time and to the times in which we live: "Be very careful, then, how you live—not as unwise but as wise, making the most of every opportunity, because the days are evil. Therefore do not be foolish, but understand what the Lord's will is" (Ephesians 5:15-17).

What is the will of God regarding time? Does God ask us to use every minute in purposeful labor? Does He speak to us of organizing our day for maximum productivity? Does God encourage short nights and long work days? What do we take as our model of a day well spent?

Time Well Spent

The account of Jesus as a guest in Martha's home is a touchstone for me. This passage has it all: challenge, instruction, encouragement, humor, and drama. I touched on this passage in chapter 4 in regard to our choices. Look again at these few brief sentences to see what Jesus has to say about spending time with Him. As usual, Jesus isn't predictable. No matter how many times I read this portion, His response is always a cannon shot, putting a hole in me. You remember the familiar paragraphs:

> *As Jesus and his disciples were on their way, he came to a village where a woman named Martha opened her home to him. She had a sister called Mary, who sat at the Lord's feet listening to what he said. But Martha was distracted by all the preparations that had to be made. She came to him and asked, "Lord, don't you care that my sister has left me to do the work by myself? Tell her to help me!"*
>
> *"Martha, Martha," the Lord answered, "you are worried and upset about many things, but only one thing is needed. Mary has chosen what is better, and it will not be taken away from her."* (Luke 10:38-42)

Mary is at leisure with her Lord—lost to time with her gaze fixed on Him. Their talk is companionable, easy. She has Him all to herself. She has not set the timer or checked her watch. Time stands still.

Mary raises a red flag in our hearts. But Martha is the kind of person we can relate to. She's busy. Martha bustles and flutters around the edges of this account, the epitome of responsibility. We can hear her clattering pots and pans in the background, rattling the silverware, and slamming cupboard doors. The noise level rises. So does her irritability. When she can bear it no more, she bursts on the scene, her fists on her hips, foot tapping. "Lord," she says, sure that He would be outraged when He realized that she was working her fingers to the bone while Mary sat idly at His feet. "Don't You care that my sister has left me to do the work by myself? Tell her to help me!"

We know that Jesus is a fair-minded man, and we think we know what He will say: "Oh! Look at the time! Please forgive us, Martha. We had no idea you were carrying the load alone. How insensitive of Me. Mary, run along and quit lazing about listening to Me."

But no! What's this? Jesus sides with Mary. "Martha, Martha, you are worried and upset about many things, but only one thing is needed. Mary has chosen what is better, and it will not be taken away from her."

What is God's will regarding our use of time? From the words of Jesus to Mary and Martha, I'd say that time communing with Him is high on the list, wouldn't you? If this is the case, be very careful, thoughtful, and deliberate in the way you live. Be wise, purposeful, and intentional, choosing how you will spend your time.

Is Time with God "Doing Nothing"?

Why is it so hard for us to accept Jesus' assessment of the situation? I believe that one of the reasons we neglect more leisurely times with the Lord is that we mistakenly think that God (and maybe our pastor and our friends) will think we're shirking our duty. We don't want to sit at Jesus' feet "doing nothing" when there is so much that needs to be done. But Jesus thinks differently. He doesn't think we're doing nothing when we spend time with Him. According to Jesus, "only one thing is needed," and it's not kitchen work, not teaching Sunday school, not having a successful career.

Jesus commends Mary for taking time to commune with Him. But that was nearly two thousand years ago, we say. Women in those days didn't have to clean the toilet, order pizza, or carpool. We dismiss life then as a "slower time" to let ourselves off the hook. Mary didn't know the demands of life that we know, we say. But then we remember frantic Martha and realize that the tendency toward busyness cuts across the centuries.

Learn from Mary. Be alert to opportunities to spend special times with God. In addition to your regular daily time with the Lord, consider occasionally meeting with Him for extended times.

Is it idleness to read, to study, to compose, to write?

Is it idleness to examine our conscience, to regulate our passions, to recall our past life, to put in order our present state, to provide wisely for the future?

Is it idleness to repent our past sins, to combat temptation and inordinate desires, to arm ourselves in advance against the proximate occasions of sin and worry, to think of death and to picture it vividly so that it may not catch us unaware?

Is it idleness to meditate on human and divine truths which alone entrall noble minds, to ponder these truths, not in haphazard daydreams but with order and concentration?

Is it idleness to raise our voices frequently by day and night in psalms, canticles, and hymns, praising God, and thanking Him for all His benefits?

Or to praise Him still more eloquently and truly by mental prayer that raises us as high as mortal man can come to the divine Majesty?

—JEAN LECLERCQ, *Alone with God*[1]

LONGER TIMES WITH GOD

Throughout the ages, God has called people to occasionally spend longer periods of time with Him. Consider three recorded incidents of people withdrawing for forty days alone with God. Twice Moses spent forty days alone with God on the mountain. In both of these cases, *God* was the *initiator* (see Exodus 24:12,18; 34:2,28).

In the New Testament, the *Holy Spirit led* Jesus into the wilderness for forty days (Matthew 4:1). The fact that God Himself pressed Jesus into this time of isolation for prayer and fasting convinces me that *He* thinks it is important. Careful study of this incident reveals how critical that forty-day desert exile was. That time alone with God prepared the way for Jesus' public ministry. The wasteland testing and proving opened the sluice for the Water of Life to flow into the land. Jesus won spiritual battles of incalculable consequence. If He had succumbed to Satan's temptations, He never would have gone to the cross.

If God doesn't think protracted time alone with Him is wasted time, why do we?

Why Spend Extended Times with God?

God called Jesus, Moses, and others apart for longer times with Him. Perhaps you sense Him calling you too. These can be times of rich fellowship with the Lord. Ponder the compelling benefits for those who once in awhile separate themselves from the clamor of daily life for extra time in God's holy presence.

Growth in Faith

Once Jesus was asked, "What must we do to do the works God requires?" He responded, "The work of God is this: to believe in the one he has sent" (John 6:28-29). God requires *belief.* "And without faith it is impossible to please God, because anyone who comes to him must believe that he exists and that he rewards those who earnestly seek him" (Hebrews 11:6).

Dawson Trotman, founder of The Navigators, was a man of faith. Once when Trotman was asked by some young people how much time he spent with the Lord, he answered, "I don't think that *time* has much to do with whether God *hears* me or not. But, I do believe that time has everything to do with *whether my faith is built up* as I pray and as I stretch out in asking. I don't believe that God will ever give those great and mighty things of Jeremiah 33:3 to those who just have their little conscience-easers or some quick prayers before jumping into bed for the night."[2] Trotman's life was characterized by *sustained* periods of prayer, alone and with other believers.

Growth in Holiness

Austin Phelps, author of the classic *The Still Hour,* concluded that *much time* with God was necessary to our progress in holiness: "It has been said that no great work in literature or in science was ever wrought by a man who did not love solitude. We may lay it down as an elemental principle of religion, that no large growth in holiness was ever gained by one who did not *take* time to be often long *alone with God*."[3]

Perspective, Direction, Planning

The women I meet with for Bible study spent a half-day alone with God together. We scattered throughout my house to meet with God privately. We had completed six weeks of study, and each of us was asking the Lord what applications we should make personally as a result of our study.

Why did we make this morning alone with God part of our Bible study? We wanted to gain perspective. That morning apart, spent listening, was like walking up the mountain as Moses did. Our previous weeks of study were stretched out in the valley below us. From the mountain we saw the pattern of God's teaching with greater clarity and were able to make appropriate responses.

Roger and I, currently in a period of transition, are plotting extra times of prayer to seek and to listen. Even Jesus found extended times with God valuable when making important decisions. He spent a night in prayer before choosing the twelve disciples (see Luke 6:12-15).

Fortification, Winning Spiritual Battles

At the end of His earthly ministry, just before He went to the cross, Jesus spent prolonged, intensive time in prayer:

> *Jesus went out as usual to the Mount of Olives, and his disciples followed him. On reaching the place, he said to them, "Pray that you will not fall into temptation." He withdrew about a stone's throw beyond them, knelt down and prayed, "Father, if you are willing, take this cup from me; yet not my will, but yours be done." An angel from heaven appeared to him and strengthened him. And being in anguish, he prayed more earnestly, and his sweat was like drops of blood falling to the ground.*
>
> *When he rose from prayer and went back to the disciples, he found them asleep, exhausted from sorrow. "Why are you sleeping?" he asked them. "Get up and pray so that you will not fall into temptation." (Luke 22:39-46)*

Jesus prayed while His disciples slept. When the soldiers came to arrest Him, He stepped forward, fortified, to meet His destiny; His disciples rubbed their sleepy eyes and fled. Jesus had warned them, "Pray that you will not fall into temptation." Life is tough.

We live behind enemy lines. Extended times of prayer shore us up for the battles we face.

Pure Enjoyment

I suspect that when Mary sat at Jesus' feet it was purely for the pleasure of His company. I think it was the same for Robert Murray M'Cheyne, who died at age twenty-nine in 1843, after a brief but fruitful ministry. His biographer's servant (in his Scottish burr) said of M'Cheyne: "He used to rise at six on the Sabbath mornin', and go to bed at twelve at night, for he said he likit to have the whole day alone with God."[4]

Longer times with God come through cultivation. They do not leap into being. They come as a person is touched by the Lord in daily quiet time and stirred to know there is more — and not only to desire it, but to discipline himself or herself to pursue it.

Who Needs Longer Times with God? We All Do!

Perhaps just weeks ago you began meeting with the Lord regularly. And now you're reading a chapter about occasionally spending *longer* times with God. These ideas are new. You wonder how you should think about trying to spend an hour with God this weekend. Think of yourself as someone hot and weary who has found a fresh-water stream. You have drunk from it. Bathed in it. Refreshed yourself in it. At first, you came to the stream every day and then wandered off to other pursuits. But more and more, you return to splash about in it throughout the day. One day, you walk in the direction of the current and find that the stream gets deeper and moves faster. You follow that bubbling stream until — what's this? — it empties into a sparkling ocean. You never dreamed there was so much more. You squint as sunlight glints like diamonds jumping on the surface of the waters. You spend the entire morning drinking, diving, kicking about, laughing, and crying at the wonder of it. You glance at your watch and realize that you have an appointment in thirty minutes. You dry your feet and go singing to your meeting. As you go, you resolve, "I must make time to do this again."

Even those who are very new to the things of Christ find extended, unhurried times with God thrilling if they have adequate direction. Years ago, my husband taught a Sunday school class on Christian basics. To wind up the quarter, we had an optional session on Saturday morning to give class members an opportunity to spend a half-day in prayer. Roger gave specific, detailed suggestions for the use of the time. Each hour was represented by a circle, which Roger divided into pie-shaped wedges of five, ten, or fifteen minutes. By following this plan, all the participants were able to spend a rejuvenating morning alone with God. (For the plan they followed, see page 140 in the Appendix.)

WHAT ABOUT FASTING?

The Bible often mentions fasting along with extended times of prayer. Fasting has several benefits:

- It allows us to give uninterrupted time to seeking God. We skip meals to focus our full attention on God.
- Weaning ourselves from food makes us aware how much our days are shaped by our physical appetites.
- We buy extra time by fasting. Food shopping, meal preparation, eating, and cleanup all take time.
- We may also fast from other things that take time, divert our eyes from God, or exert control over our appetites. For example, you may determine to fast from TV for a week and spend that time in prayer and Bible study. On occasion, you may even fast from a night's regular sleep for special prayer.

How to Spend Extended Time with God

It was New Year's Eve. My parents headed out the door to celebrate with family friends; I was staying home to pray out the old year and pray in the new. I placed a candle, a clock, and my Bible on the seat of a dining room chair and knelt on a pillow before my makeshift "altar." It was eight o'clock when I began. I prayed and prayed. All prayed out, I lifted my head and stared at the clock: 8:15. I had prayed for only fifteen minutes! I was eight months into my life as a believer in Jesus and not ready for four-plus hours in prayer by myself. Over time, daily meetings with the Lord enlarged my capacity.

DATE WITH GOD

Perhaps your capacity for God has increased too. Fifteen minutes has expanded into half an hour or an hour. You long for more time, but you feel limited by your current circumstances. Consider scheduling a special date with God. With prior planning you may be able to carve out an extra hour or two. If you have children, perhaps your spouse or a friend could care for them for a two-hour period while you meet with God. At another time you could reciprocate. I remember suggesting to a mother with three preschool children that she trade child care one morning a week with her friend. She questioned the idea: "My three drive me crazy. What would I do with her three added to the soup?"

"Give it a try," I encouraged. She later told me that the morning she kept all six children was her easiest morning of the week. The children entertained one another. Besides that blessing she had a quiet, uninterrupted, leisurely morning with the Lord on the day her friend kept all the children.

Whatever your present situation, consider marking out a special date with God. Begin praying and thinking about the time as soon as you write it on your calendar. Ask God where He'd like to have the date and if He has anything special in mind for the time. He will guide you. Even if you don't sense that He has spoken directly, He is leading. He responds to seeking. Lay out a general plan for the time. Sometimes as I plan, I open to the contents page of my Bible and ask the Lord to show me where to read.

Don't squander the time you set apart for your date. Decide ahead of time where you'll go. (Many people find it advantageous to leave the distractions of home.) Gather your Bible, notebook, and pen and place them by the door or in the car. Use the time in transit to begin preparing your heart. If you are walking to the park or coffeeshop, sing or review Bible verses as you go. If you are driving, consider a praise tape or the preparation of silence.

These special dates often follow different lines than my daily times. I usually bring my Bible, song book, sometimes a devotional book, and always my pen and notebook. I may end up using all of them or none of them. I may walk and sing and listen as I weave here and there through a park. Another time, God may bring clarity to a confusing situation, and I sit like a scribe writing in my notebook, capturing perceptions, jotting responses, questions, requests, thanksgivings, and praises. Sometimes I read through large portions of the Bible without interruption. This kind of reading makes me feel like Moses standing on Mount Nebo seeing the Promised Land stretched out in the valley below. I am reminded of the big picture and where I fit into it.

A SAMPLE HALF-DAY WITH GOD

45 minutes in heart preparation: singing and reading in the Psalms.

15 minutes in quiet listening.

1 hour of reading, say, the book of James. Sometimes you may read through without stopping to ponder. Other times, you may feel the Lord's hand prompting you to stop and camp on a particular verse. Feel no compulsion to hurry on or to finish the book. Stay there until the Lord releases you to move on. If you read through without pause, circle around and read the book again. Every reading will yield its fruit. Jot down thoughts in your notebook.

1 hour to pray for family members, friends, and others in your circle of concern. Hold each one up to the Lord and ask, "How are they doing, Lord? How should I pray for them? Is there any action I should take?" Make notes in your notebook for future reference.

1 hour of reviewing past quiet time pages to review what God has spoken to you about day by day. God calls His people to *remember.* "Remember how the LORD your God led you all the way in the desert these forty years, to humble you and to test you in order to know what was in your heart, whether or not you would keep his commands. . . . Be careful that you do not forget the LORD your God, failing to observe his commands, his laws and his decrees that I am giving you this day" (Deuteronomy 8:2,11).

As you review, the comfort, challenge, and instruction of preceding days will touch your life again. Record insights and applications.

End the time expressing gratitude to the Lord.

HALF-DAY WITH THE LORD

As your capacity for God increases and as your circumstances allow, consider blocking out a half-day to spend alone with God. Once you've allotted the time, pray for a prepared heart and sensitivity to the Lord's voice. Choose a place. Assemble Bible, notebook, pen, and anything else (song book, devotional, et cetera) you want to take. Plan ahead for your use of this time.

PERSONAL RETREAT

You may associate the term "retreat" with a conference taken with others. Personal retreat, however, is a private getaway for you and God alone. It may be a significant chunk of a day or more. When our children were older, my husband and I often reserved vacation mornings for time with God. The children would sleep in and then get their own breakfast and occupy themselves until lunch time. Then the whole family would trek off to do something. As a result, vacations refreshed us spiritually as well as physically and benefited the entire family.

PURPOSE AND BENEFITS OF EXTENDED TIMES WITH GOD

- Focus your whole attention on God
- Commune with God (listening and speaking)
- Inquire of God
- Remember the work and words of God
- Praise and thank God
- Intercede for others
- Examine your conscience
- Reflect on your conversion and journey
- Rethink your use of time, your priorities, your direction, your character
- Repent and set new directions by His grace
- Revisit His promises and take fresh hold of them
- Review past journal entries
- Remember that you are mortal and will soon face God

▦SUMMARY▦

God wants us to spend time sitting at His feet. He says time with Him is "the one thing needed." Respond to the stirrings you have to spend some longer times with God. He is the initiator of your desire. Take extra time with God to grow in faith and holiness and to gain fresh perspective.

▦MAKING IT PERSONAL▦

Mark on your calendar a special date with God of at least one hour. Begin praying about that time. Lay out a rough plan of how you'll spend the time. Gather anything you want to take with you in advance. Enjoy!

▦REFLECTION AND DISCUSSION QUESTIONS▦

1. What idea from this chapter would you like to give more thought to? Why?

2. Read Exodus 24 and 34 (accounts of Moses spending forty days apart with God on two different occasions). Note who initiated the time. What was the purpose? What were the results?

3. Getting away for forty days when you are the leader of a country isn't simple. How did Moses handle the logistics of being away (see Exodus 24:13-14)? How might you apply this idea?

4. What is the biggest obstacle you face in getting a date alone with God? What creative solutions might you try?

5. In what ways do you think an extra block of uninterrupted time with God might benefit your spiritual life?

6. What are your plans for putting a special date with God on the calendar?

NINE

A Lifetime of Quiet Times

SO FAR, WE'VE DISCUSSED QUIET TIME SOLELY IN TERMS OF YOUR individual relationship with God: two people meeting together every day. Just you and God. In this final chapter, we'll consider the fact that God calls us all to touch the world in which we live. Our life in Christ must flow out of us to others. Remember that Christian service, or ministry, is not what you do for God, but what *He does through you.*

JESUS PASSES THE TORCH

The passion of God's heart is that we might know Him. To this end, Jesus came to earth. The Son of God left the glory He shared with the Father so that He might reveal the Father here on earth and reconcile us to Him. Jesus' prayer in John 17 is, in one sense, a ministry debriefing. He reports to the Father: "I have . . . completed the work you gave me to do" (John 17:4). Jesus' work before He went to the cross was to reveal the Father (verse 6) and give us the Father's words (verse 8). Now, as the Cross looms, Jesus passes the torch to us. The task of revealing the Father now falls to us. Jesus prays: "As you sent me into the world, I have sent them into the world" (John 17:18).

Jesus continues His prayer:

"My prayer is not for them alone. I pray also for those who
will believe in me through their message, that all of them
may be one, Father, just as you are in me and I am in you.
May they also be in us so that the world may believe that
you have sent me. I have given them the glory that you
gave me, that they may be one as we are one: I in them and
you in me. May they be brought to complete unity to let the
world know that you sent me and have loved them even as
you have loved me." (John 17:20-23)

Jesus delegates His work on earth—revealing the Father and
reconciling people to Him—to those who believe, generation after
generation. It's a big job. How are we to do it? Jesus prays that we
will follow His pattern. He lived His life on earth *in union* with the
Father, allowing the Father to express His thoughts, words, and
actions through Him (see John 8:26-29). Now Jesus prays that we
will live connected to Him so that He can express His thoughts,
words, and actions through us.

Quiet time daily affirms your oneness with Christ. Your time with
the Lord reminds you that Jesus prayed for you to live in union with
Him, just as He lived in union with the Father. Quiet time is the pause
to remember afresh that by faith and obedience you abide in Christ
and He abides in you (see John 14:20). Your quiet time sets the direction for a life of devotion, surrender, obedience, and service.

A UNIFIED LIFE

Your union with Jesus produces a unified life. This is integrity,
wholeness. The line between sacred and secular in your life is
erased. As you live in oneness with Christ, He expresses His life
through you. He touches your world. All of life becomes holy. All
things are done for the glory of God. This is the kind of life that
reveals the Father to the world you rub shoulders with every day.

No practice is more essential to living a holy, well-integrated life
than a regular, well-established, tender devotional life. It is in the daily

and deliberate practice of placing oneself in the presence of God and in the hearing of His Word that a unified life becomes reality. Clergyman Jeremy Taylor (1613–1667) wrote that through the devotional life a person moves toward "the sanctification of the whole man."

Daniel is a good example of one who lived attached to God, expecting God to work through him. His habit of quiet time was a well-established part of his life—and it showed. "Now when Daniel learned that the decree had been published, he went home to his upstairs room where the windows opened toward Jerusalem. Three times a day he got down on his knees and prayed, giving thanks to his God, just as he had done before" (Daniel 6:10).

Daniel had a time, a place, and a plan. But the phrase, "just as he had done before," is the muscle holding those bones together. The practice of meeting with God gave strength and structure to Daniel's life. If you stood in God's place and looked down on Daniel's life, you would see a pattern woven into Daniel's days. You couldn't miss that praying figure at his window three times a day, year after year. Others were aware of it too. His fellow workers, jealous of his success, knew of Daniel's unwavering devotion to his God and made that their point of attack. Daniel's spiritual life made an impression on the king as well. Twice in the account of Daniel's life, the king mentioned "the God . . . you serve continually" (Daniel 6:16,20).

Daniel was a man of exceptional competence and character. That was obvious to all. Just as apparent was his unshakable commitment to fellowship with His God. Daniel habitually gave God his time and attention, and those around him could see the fruit in his life.

GOD WORKING THROUGH HIS PEOPLE

The prophet Jeremiah also established a pattern of daily fellowship with God. He met with God morning after morning and then faced an impossibly frustrating task. Every day for twenty-three years, Jeremiah proclaimed the Word of God to an unresponsive, hostile people. He knew *beforehand* that they would not listen. Yet he did not grudgingly shuffle out to once again preach to unhearing ears. No! Jeremiah went to work every day fortified by what went on *inside of him* as a result of his time with God. God's Word was a fire in Jeremiah's mouth (see Jeremiah 5:14, 23:28-29) and a fire shut up in his bones (see Jeremiah 20:9). Day after day, Jeremiah went out carrying that fire inside. What he heard from God he faithfully preached to a people whose spiritual hormones were set on adultery.

What motivated Jeremiah and kept him going was not the job satisfaction of moving up in the business, seeing lives changed, or getting a glowing fitness review. He was motivated by hearing God every day. He listened. He ate: "When your words came, I ate them; they were my joy and my heart's delight, for I bear your name, O LORD God Almighty" (Jeremiah 15:16). That's what enabled him to carry out his mission with passion.

Like Daniel and Jeremiah, what goes on day by day in the closet affects your public life. Oswald Chambers says that if your relationship with Jesus is right,

> then whatever circumstances you are in, and whoever you meet day by day, He is pouring rivers of living water through you and it is of His mercy that He does not let you know it. When once you are related to God by salvation and sanctification, remember that wherever you are, you are put there by God; and by the reaction of your life on the circumstances around you, you will fulfill God's purpose, as long as you keep in the light as God is in the light.[1]

You, too, are a channel for the work of God. When you believed, you were united to Christ. As you live in that union (see John 15:1-6), His life streams through you like sap running through the veins of a plant, nourishing every part, bearing fruit. Your life is really *His life* expressing itself *through you*. As you remain attached to Christ, He does His work in the world through you. Your quiet time is what keeps you intimately connected to Christ.

You draw near to God for His touch, and the life of God in you touches others. You come as a learner, a disciple—and through you others learn of Him. God spreads through us the fragrance of the knowledge of Christ (see 2 Corinthians 2:14). "For we are to God the aroma of Christ among those who are being saved and those who are perishing. To the one we are the smell of death; to the other, the fragrance of life. And who is equal to such a task?" (2 Corinthians 2:15-16). We aren't conscious of it happening. We're not supposed to be. It is a work of God for His glory. Oswald Chambers wrote:

> If you want to be of use to God, get rightly related to
> Jesus Christ and He will make you of use unconsciously
> every minute you live.[2]

How can God pour His life through us if we're not attached to Him? How can our lives be a testimony if we don't live in vital oneness with Him? How can we reveal the Father if we haven't taken the time to get to know Him ourselves? How can we give others the Father's words if we neglect them in our own lives? How can we help another know God better if we are careless about our own time with God? Quiet time helps us stay rightly related to God so that He can make us of use unconsciously every minute we live.

HELPING ANOTHER PERSON BEGIN QUIET TIME

One of life's greatest joys is helping another person know God better through quiet time. Whether the person is just beginning to walk with Christ or has been a believer for many years, nothing will make Christ's life in them more real and efficacious than daily quiet times. Because quiet time is personal and individual at every stage, think carefully about the person you are encouraging toward quiet time.

1. What is his or her background? Churched or unchurched?
2. What is his or her knowledge of the Bible?
3. What is his or her stage of life and circumstance?
4. What is his or her spiritual appetite?

Some years ago, a pastor I had never met called and asked if I would help a young woman he had just led to faith in Jesus Christ. Mary was bright, direct, and free-spirited. I liked her right away. As we got acquainted, I discovered that she didn't attend church and had little knowledge of the Bible. She seemed spiritually alive and hungry.

We talked about her decision to give herself to Christ and the wonderful, new life she was beginning. I related something of my experience with Christ and how meeting with the Lord every morning helped me understand how to live this new life. I encouraged her to spend time with God every day too.

To get Mary started, I gave her a spiral-bound notebook and asked if she had a Bible. Her background and circumstances demanded a simple approach. I explained to Mary that the Bible was divided into what happened before Jesus came to earth as a man (Old Testament) and what happened after (New Testament). The first four books of the New Testament tell about the time Jesus lived on earth. I recommended she start reading in the Gospel of Mark. "Take a moment to ask God to teach you before you read," I suggested. "Then read slowly through a chapter. When you finish reading, write out your favorite verse from that chapter into your notebook. Next week when we get together, bring your notebook and Bible with you." The assignment was non-threatening—no right or wrong answers, merely her favorite verse—but it did force a beginning in meditation. Mary had to consider which verse she liked best. Copying the verse allowed for further thought.

The following week Mary came with notebook, Bible, and lots of questions. She'd had a quiet time every day and read aloud to me the verses she had copied into her notebook. I probed, "Mary, tell me, why did you choose that verse?"

I offered these instructions for the second week: "This week, after you write your favorite verse, write a sentence or two of why you chose that verse." In small increments, I was guiding Mary into thinking more deeply and personally about what she was reading. I also encouraged her to take a few minutes each day to thank God for her new life and to ask for His help. I looked forward to the times when Mary and I would visit about that week's quiet times.

Unlike Mary, Melody, a college freshman, grew up in church and had a basic knowledge of the Bible. She had heard about quiet time in a general way and had made various attempts over the years. "I know it's important, but I can't seem to keep it going more than three days in a row," she agonized. For Melody, I suggested the 4R approach discussed in chapter 2.

MY PART IN HELPING SOMEONE ELSE WITH QUIET TIME

Tell her why—motivate
Show her how—instruct
Keep her going—problem-solve, enrich, adapt the
assignments
Help her pass it on—encourage her to share with others what
she is learning; help her eventually help
others begin to meet with the Lord

A CHANGED LIFE

Before I speak at a retreat, my husband often asks, "What do you hope will happen in the lives of these people as a result of the weekend?" Roger brought to my attention that, regardless of the theme of the conference, my answer is always the same: "I want them to meet with God in quiet time."

This book was Roger's idea. "This is a passion for you," he said. It's my passion because, as I look back on my life, nothing has made more of a difference.

My Own Lifetime of Quiet Times

When I surrendered my life to Christ, I had very limited church exposure and was thoroughly ignorant of the Bible. I lacked a spiritual language to speak to God or to share my love for Him with others. My prayers were mostly wordless, basking in a love that would not let me go. As I read the Bible, I began to catch glimmers of the new life that was mine. Prayer found words. I sought God in quietness and solitude. It wasn't a discipline; it was a love affair. That morning time with God, which began nearly forty years ago, has been central to my life ever since.

But not without the usual struggles. I've known times when it seemed God disappeared, leaving only a shadow of His presence behind; times when days were so full and pressured that I wondered if eliminating quiet time might be a temporary way to lighten the load; times when we lived overseas and babies came one after another, crowding into the home that already swelled with extra adults who lived as part of our family. I've had quiet times while I nursed a baby. I've met with God, or at least tried to, when I was so tired my brain felt like hamburger.

You may be asking, "Why grind it out? God understands that some times in life are too demanding to add one more thing."

But I kept working at meeting with God because our two lives are merged together. I can't separate myself from Him. His Spirit lives inside of me; His life is now my life. I keep coming because I can't help it.

Sometimes I've wondered as I work on this book, "Who am I to write a book on meeting with God? Certainly my times with the Lord aren't anything to be held up as a model for others. I've stumbled along, sometimes not even remembering anything from a quiet time I had just hours ago."

But I kept writing because I want to encourage you in what I'm certain is the most important practice in life. I kept writing because even if you end up like me, forty years down the road and feeling like you're just beginning, we will both be heading in the right direction—toward the heart of God.

This is the last chapter. In one way we part company. In another way, I hope this book will be an ongoing resource for you. Some ideas you passed over in a first reading might be applicable to a later situation. Examples of how others have handled their times with the Lord will remind you that one's relationship with God is personal and unique. The Appendix develops some ideas too lengthy to deal with in the body of the book, ideas to enrich quiet times far into the future.

This is a good time to think about developing your relationship with God. Where will you go from here? What have you learned? Where are you in your understanding, experience, and consistency of meeting with the Lord?

Consider the apostle Paul, who at approximately sixty years of age expressed the passion of his life in this way: "I want to know Christ and the power of his resurrection and the fellowship of sharing in his sufferings, becoming like him in his death" (Philippians 3:10). This familiar passage sums up the goal and direction of his life. It also serves as a heartfelt prayer for all of us that follow—that we might know Christ!

A Prayer for Quiet Time

What can I give You in gratitude? Nothing, but myself. I offer my life to You as an empty vessel for Your purposes and glory. Cleanse me. Possess me. Fill me. Use me. Make me what You had in mind when You created me and chose me as Your own.

Lord, I confess my bent toward unbelief, pride, and rebellion. Help me to trust You today, to believe that everything You say is thoroughly true and right and good. Help me live as the Lord Jesus did, in total dependence on the Father. Give me a heart that wants to obey in all things.

Lord, I am in You and You are in me. Help me stay attached to You all day, connected, one with You. May I hear Your Spirit's promptings and respond. May Your life flow through me, fully expressing Yourself to me and through me. Keep my heart tender and attuned to You that I might live as a vessel of Your tender mercies to those I meet, and that I might work faithfully and diligently as unto You in all my work today.

Make Your will in all things clear and give me grace to do it.

Above all, may Christ be formed in me. In all things may You be enthroned in my heart for Your glory and the furtherance of Your kingdom.

⠿SUMMARY⠿

Resolve to keep space in your life for God for the rest of your life. Live attached to Jesus so that He can manifest Himself in your life and influence others through you. Introduce others to the joy of meeting regularly with God.

⠿MAKING IT PERSONAL⠿

Determine your plan for the next month of quiet times. Write your plan here as a reminder.

⠿DISCUSSION AND REFLECTION QUESTIONS⠿

1. This is a good time to assess what you've learned: from the book, from your quiet times, from others in your discussion group, if you have one.

2. What attitudes, choices, and decisions are helping you be more consistent in quiet time? What hindrances are you facing?

3. Can you name someone whom you might get started in meeting with God? What factors (his or her knowledge of the Bible, circumstances, and so on) would you have to take into consideration? Customize a plan for that person.

4. How have regular quiet times made a difference in your life?

Appendix

A "PEACE-GIVING" EXERCISE (CHAPTER 3)

Some years ago, our house was broken into several times while we were at church. I felt anxious whenever I returned to the house alone, wondering if I might face an intruder. In my quiet time, God brought to mind thoughts about who He is and what He is like. I held up one characteristic of God at a time and looked at my circumstance through the filter of that attribute. This is how it looked:

BEHOLD YOUR GOD

Problem: The break-ins

God Is All-Knowing
God knows who did it, why they did it, what He wants us to learn from it, how this can bring Him glory, and how the burglar can be caught. God knows how upset this makes me feel. God knows how much we can take.

God Is All-Powerful
God can stop the burglaries. He can sustain us even if they last until we die. He can use it for good in our lives, the burglar's life, other Christians' lives, and to promote the gospel (Philippians 1:12). He can protect us and our stuff, or He can take it all.

continued on next page

God Is All-Present

God watches us and the burglar (see Proverbs 15:3). He is with me even if I should be confronted personally by an enemy. I need not fear; God is near.

God Loves Me

He loves us, and nothing may touch us except as His love allows it. The break-ins are part of our lives because He loves us. God loves the burglar too.

God Is My Father

A father teaches and disciplines his children. A father provides, comforts, explains. Thank You that You are giving meaning to the burglaries and using them in our lives. Thank You that You are drawing us closer to You through the burglaries.

SPIRITUAL APPETIZERS (CHAPTER 5)

From time to time when you hit a spiritual dry spell, you'll notice that your spiritual appetite is lagging behind. Try an appetizer to get you hungering after God and His Word again. Here are some ideas to sink your teeth into.

Appetizer 1

Joshua 1:8—"Do not let this Book of the Law depart from your mouth; meditate on it day and night, so that you may be careful to do everything written in it. Then you will be prosperous and successful."

Meditate on this verse. As you do so, insert the following dictionary definitions into the verse.

let: allow, permit

depart: to go away, set forth, leave; to vary, deviate

mouth: opening through which any container is filled or emptied

meditate: to reflect upon, ponder, contemplate; to plan or intend in the mind

careful: cautious in thought, speech or action; circumspect, prudent, thorough, conscientious

do: to perform or execute; to carry out the requirements of; fulfill; complete
prosperous: having success; flourishing, well off
successful: achieving something desired, planned, attempted

Appetizer 2

John, a Canadian friend, rewrites verses inserting personal pronouns. This is how Joshua 1:8 might read: *I will not let this Book of the Law depart from my mouth; I will meditate on it day and night, so that I may be careful to do everything written in it. Then I will be prosperous and successful.*

Consider the implications of this personal approach for your life. What would your life look like if each phrase in Joshua 1:8 were true in your life? What is one step you could take in that direction?

Appetizer 3

I find putting two verses side by side and allowing them to shine their light on each other makes a tasty treat.

Example A

Joshua 1:8—"Do not let this Book of the Law depart from your mouth; meditate on it day and night, so that you may be careful to do everything written in it. Then you will be prosperous and successful."

Job 23:12—"I have not departed from the commands of his lips; I have treasured the words of his mouth more than my daily bread."

Example B

Joshua 1:8—"Do not let this Book of the Law depart from your mouth; meditate on it day and night, so that you may be careful to do everything written in it. Then you will be prosperous and successful."

Jeremiah 15:16—"When your words came, I ate them; they were my joy and my heart's delight, for I bear your name, O LORD God Almighty."

(Create similar appetizers to nibble on to stimulate your appetite.)

GET PHYSICAL: STATIONS OF THE CROSS (CHAPTER 7)

Our Lord helps us understand spiritual truth by using concrete terms. For example, Jesus calls Himself a Shepherd, Living Water, a Vine, a Bridegroom. Jesus uses the tangible to help us grasp invisible realities. He tells us to take bread and wine as representations of His body and blood. In the Old Testament, God commands that the tabernacle be made to strict specification because every part reveals deep spiritual truth.

Consider including a more physical approach in your private worship from time to time. For example, you might incorporate a candle, flashlight, or lamp as part of your meditation on Jesus as the light of the world. Allow the next wedding you attend to enlarge your reflection on Jesus as the bridegroom. In fact, every physical object can enrich your understanding and appreciation of spiritual truth.

Roman Catholics assign fourteen physical locations to represent Jesus' journey to the cross. These stations may be designated within the church itself or outside. Some retreat centers create a trail through the woods where the worshiper can pause and think about what Christ faced at each point. The Catholic model comes from Scripture and tradition and ends with Jesus on the cross. I prefer a model based only on Scripture and ending with the resurrection and ascension.

There is great value in frequently concentrating your meditation on Jesus' sacrifice. The Cross is the pivot on which your life in Christ turns. When you first started your walk with Christ, you paid little attention to the road. But in time you noticed that the road is always present. Every road we walk with Jesus originates at the Cross. To deepen your understanding and appreciation of the Cross, create your own "Stations of the Cross" within your home, yard, or in a nearby park.

▪ Read again and again the last chapters of each gospel.
▪ Write down what you feel are the significant events.

Using your list of events as a guide, assign a physical location as the place where you will stand to meditate on that event. You may move through the entire course pausing at each station or you may spend most of your time at one particular spot and use the rest of the course as context. Whatever your pace, complete the route to remind yourself that He died in your place, He is risen and returning.

HOW I CREATED AND USED MY "STATIONS OF THE CROSS"

I spent quiet times soaking in the gospel accounts of the events surrounding the Cross (see Matthew 26–28, Mark 14–16, Luke 22–24, John 18–20).

On index cards I copied small chunks of Scripture from those portions. I carry these with me as I pause at each station to contemplate the events of Jesus' last days on earth. Each card records some event. For example, the soldiers mock Jesus (see Matthew 27:27-31) or Jesus' prayer in Gethsemane (see Mark 14:32-36).

I designate four physical locations (stations) where I will pause and consider the Lord's work on the Cross and its implications in my life:

1. An event that immediately precedes the Cross, such as Jesus predicting Peter's denial (see Mark 14:27-31) or Jesus finding His disciples asleep instead of praying (see Mark 14:37-42).

2. Some aspect of the Cross itself, such as the insults Jesus faced (see Mark 14:25-32).

3. Some aspect of the resurrection (see Luke 24:1-6).

4. Jesus giving me the Great Commission (see Matthew 28:19-20) and ascending.

I stand in one location (for example, by a tree) and think about an event that occurred before Jesus was crucified. As I walk to the next point (perhaps a rock), I imagine myself following Jesus on His way to Golgotha. I linger there, engaging myself (by imagining myself as Jesus or as a spectator to the crucifixion) as fully as I can. At each different point I use an index card to help me focus. The walk from point to point is as meaningful as the stations themselves, reminding me of the total picture.

REFRESHING THROUGH "RE-" WORDS (CHAPTER 7)

Jesus fulfilled the prophecy about Himself written in Isaiah: "A bruised reed he will not break, and a smoldering wick he will not snuff out" (Isaiah 42:3, Matthew 12:20). It is good to know that Jesus cares about the bruised and broken because almost everybody has been battered by life. All of us are in need of His redeeming work and of a host of other "re-" words.

When you come before the Lord in prayer, use this list of "re-" words to put you in touch with your need, His compassionate care, and the need to extend grace and care to the needy world around you. For example, choose a word from the list below that speaks to your need and look up the verses suggested. Meditate on these verses. You may even want to copy them into your notebook as a resource for future reference. The exact "re-" word may not be found in the verse but the idea will be there.

Reassurance—Jeremiah 29:11, Hebrews 13:5, 1 John 5:13-15

Rebirth—John 1:13, John 3:3-8, 1 Peter 1:23

Rebound—Psalm 37:24-25, Psalm 145:14, Proverbs 24:16

Rebuild—Isaiah 58:9-12

Rebuke—Proverbs 9:8, 2 Timothy 3:16, 2 Timothy 4:2, Revelation 3:19-20

Recapture—Revelation 2:4-5

Receive—Matthew 7:8, John 1:12, Acts 1:8, Acts 20:35, Revelation 4:11

Recommit—1 Kings 8:61, 2 Chronicles 16:9, Psalm 37:5, Proverbs 16:3, 1 Peter 4:19

Reconcile—Matthew 5:24, Romans 5:10, 2 Corinthians 5:18

Reconsider—Psalm 107:43, Isaiah 41:20, Philippians 3:8

Recount—Psalm 40:5, Psalm 71:15, Psalm 139:17-18

Recover, Recuperate—Isaiah 38:15-19

Redeem—Psalm 71:23, Psalm 107:2, Galatians 3:13

continued on next page

Refill—Psalm 16:11, Psalm 81:10, Romans 15:13

Refine—Psalm 12:6, Daniel 11:35, Zechariah 13:9

Reflect—Exodus 33:11, Exodus 34:29-35, 2 Corinthians 3:18

Refresh— Exodus 31:17, Acts 3:19, Romans 15:32,
      Philemon 20

Refuge— Psalm 36:7, Psalm 46:1, Psalm 57:1-2, Proverbs
      14:26

Rejoice—Psalm 5:11, Psalm 13:5-6, Luke 10:20, Philippians
      4:4, James 1:9

Release—Isaiah 61:1, John 8:31-36, Romans 6:22

Relinquish—Job 1:21-22, Daniel 3:28, Luke 9:23-25

Rely—2 Chronicles 13:18, Proverbs 3:5-6, Isaiah 50:10

Remember—Deuteronomy 8:2, Psalm 77:11-12, Ephesians
      2:11-13, Revelation 3:3

Remove—Ezekiel 36:26, Matthew 7:3-5, Matthew 17:20

Renew—Psalm 51:10, Isaiah 40:31, Philippians 4:10

Renounce—2 Corinthians 4:2

Repair—Job 5:17-18, Isaiah 61:1-4

Repay—Psalm 116:12, Romans 12:19, 1 Peter 3:9

Repent—Psalm 37:27, Jeremiah 18:7-8, Matthew 3:8,
      Romans 2:4, 2 Corinthians 7:9-10

Replenish—Jeremiah 31:25

Rescue—Psalm 97:10, Daniel 3:28-29, Daniel 6:26-27

Resist—James 4:7, 1 Peter 5:9

Rest—Psalm 91:1, Jeremiah 6:16, Matthew 11:28

Restore—Psalm 23:3, Psalm 51:10-12, Jeremiah 31:18,
      Joel 2:25

Return—Jeremiah 15:19, Joel 2:12-14

Reveal—Deuteronomy 4:29, Isaiah 65:1, Jeremiah 29:13,
      John 14:21

Revere—Malachi 4:2, Hebrews 12:28-29

HOW TO SPEND A HALF-DAY IN PRAYER (CHAPTER 8)

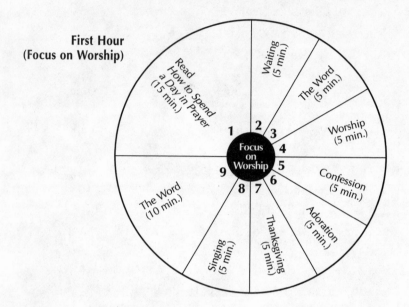

First Hour
(Focus on Worship)

Explanation:

1. Read the booklet *How to Spend a Day in Prayer* by Lorne Sanny (NavPress).
2. Take time to allow the Lord to make you conscious of His presence.
3. Read Psalm 139.
4. Psalm 139 reveals the omniscience, omnipresence, and omnipotence of God. Worship His greatness as revealed in this passage.
5. Pray Psalm 139:23-24. Allow God to bring to your attention any issue that needs to be confessed. Make a note to yourself if it requires any action on your part, such as confessing to someone else besides God.
6. Use the names of God to further worship Him.
7. Thank the Lord for all He has done for you.
8. Use a favorite hymn or two to express your love to the Lord.
9. Read and pray over Psalm 103 and 104.

Second Hour
(Focus on Intercession)

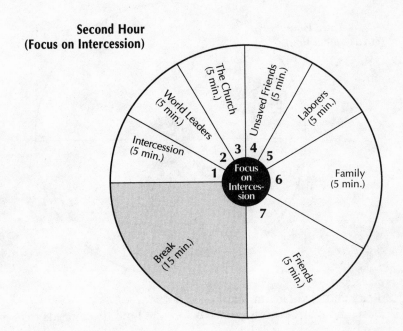

Explanation:

1. Pray for others. Through prayer, you can touch lives anywhere in the world. Quiet your heart. Ask the Holy Spirit to guide your requests for others.
2. Pray for the leaders of our country and the other nations of the world (see 1 Timothy 2:1-2).
3. Pray for the church, in the United States and internationally (see Ephesians 5:26-27). Remember those who are poor, persecuted, isolated.
4. Pray for your unsaved friends (see 1 Timothy 2:3-6).
5. Pray for the world's full-time laborers for Christ (see Colossians 1:9-11; 4:6,17). Remember your pastoral staff and missionaries you know.
6. Pray for your family (see Genesis 18:19).
7. Pray for your special friends.
8. You may find it helpful to complete this second hour by taking a fifteen-minute break. Get up and move around, take a short walk, or get a drink.

**Third Hour
(Focus on Petition)**

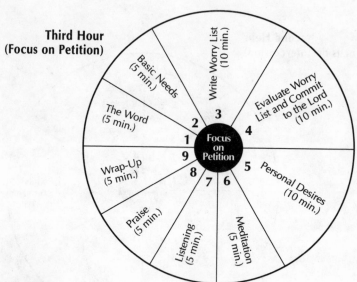

Explanation:

1. Read and meditate on Matthew 6:6-15.

2. Based on Matthew 6:11, place before the Lord those needs that are basic to your well-being.

3. Make a list of your current conflicts, problems, concerns, or frustrations—no matter how small. Ask God to reveal anything else that is a point of concern.

4. Go through the list to determine if there's anything you can do to resolve the issues. If there's nothing you can do for some, pray about them. Then make a list of things you plan to do specifically to help resolve them.

5. Talk to the Lord about things that are not needs but that you would like Him to do (see Psalm 37:4-5).

6. Read and meditate on Matthew 7:7-12.

7. Allow God, through the Holy Spirit, to speak to your heart. Be silent. List or respond to anything He has to say.

8. Acknowledge His greatness and ability to do all you have asked and more (see Psalm 100:4, Matthew 6:13).

9. As you conclude, make notes about any strong impressions from this time. For example, a particular scripture may have come to you with special power, or God may have given you an idea for solving a problem you're facing. Now, go into your day confident of His presence with you.

Notes

Chapter 1
1. Andrew Bonar, *Robert Murray M'Cheyne* (London: The Banner of Truth Trust, 1962), p. 30.
2. Gerard Manley Hopkins, "Thou Mastering Me God," *Hopkins* (New York: Knopf, 1995) pp. 98-99 by permission of David Campbell Publishers Ltd.

Chapter 2
1. C. S. Lewis, *The Weight of Glory* (New York: Macmillan, 1949), p. 52.
2. Oswald Chambers, *My Utmost for His Highest* (Westwood, NJ: Dodd, Mead, 1963), p. 167.

Chapter 3
1. A.W. Tozer, *The Knowledge of the Holy* (London: James Clarke & Co., 1961), p. 7.
2. Bernard of Clairvaux, *Great Devotional Classics* (Nashville: The Upper Room, 1952), p. 8.

Chapter 4
1. Annie Dillard, *The Writing Life* (New York: Harper & Row, 1989), p. 32.
2. Emilie Griffin, *Wilderness Time* (San Francisco: HarperSanFrancisco, 1997), p. 2.
3. A.W. Tozer, *The Divine Conquest* (New York: Revell, MCML), p. 22.
4. Alfred Barrett, "Incense," from *Mint by Night*, as quoted in *The Crown Treasury of Relevant Quotations* (1979), Crown Publishing, p. 489.

Chapter 5
1. Joseph Cardinal Bernardin, *The Gift of Peace* (Chicago: Loyola, 1997), p. 97.
2. C. S. Lewis, *Mere Christianity* (New York: Macmillan, 1952), p. 180.
3. Arthur Porritt, *John Henry Jowett* (London: Hodder & Stoughton, 1924), p. 232.
4. Charles E. Hummel, *Tyranny of the Urgent* (Downer's Grove: InterVarsity, 1967), p. 9.
5. Quoted by John Henry Jowett, *The School of Calvary* (London: James Clarke & Co., 1910), p. 24.
6. John Knox, *Great Devotional Classics* (Nashville: The Upper Room, 1962), p. 12.

Chapter 6
1. Henri J. M. Nouwen, *Bread for the Journey* (San Francisco: HarperSanFrancisco, 1997), April 27.
2. Quoted by Sophy Burnham, *For Writers Only* (New York: Ballantine Books, 1994), p. 42.
3. John Wesley, *Great Devotional Classics* (Nashville: The Upper Room, 1962), p. 11.

Chapter 7

1. *The Golden Treasury of Puritan Quotations,* compiled by I. D. E. Thomas (Chicago: Moody, 1975), p. 75.
2. Andrew Bonar, *Robert Murray M'Cheyne* (London: The Banner of Truth Trust, 1962), p. 26.
3. Francis Asbury, *Great Devotional Classics* (Nashville: The Upper Room, 1962), p. 8.
4. Richard J. Foster, *Celebration of Discipline* (San Francisco: Harper & Row, 1978), p. 90.
5. Rev. J. C. Macauley, "Thyself," as quoted in *Wuest's Commentary on 1 Peter* (Grand Rapids: Eerdmans,1956), p. 28.
6. George MacDonald, "The Castle: A Parable," *The Gifts of the Christ Child* (Grand Rapids: Eerdmans, 1973), p. 284.
7. Chrysostom, *The World's Great Sermons, Vol. 1,* compiled by Grenville Kleiser (London: Funk & Wagnalls, 1908), p. 26.
8. MacDonald, p. 284.
9. Georges Bernanos, as quoted in *Theological Notebook, Vol. 1,* by Donald G. Bloesch (Colorado Springs: Helmers & Howard, 1989), p. 31.

Chapter 8

1. Jean Leclercq, *Alone with God,* translated by Elizabeth McCabe (New York: Farrar, Straus and Cudahy, 1961), pp. 84-85.
2. Robert D. Foster, *The Navigator* (Colorado Springs: NavPress, 1983), p. 30.
3. Austin Phelps, *The Still Hour* (Edinburgh: The Banner of Truth Trust, 1974), p. 64.
4. Andrew Bonar, *Robert Murray M'Cheyne* (London: The Banner of Truth Trust, 1962), p. 4.

Chapter 9

1. Oswald Chambers, *My Utmost for His Highest* (Westwood, NJ: Dodd, Mead, 1963), p. 243.
2. Chambers, p. 139.

OTHER DEVOTIONAL AND PRAYER RESOURCES

The staff at any Christian bookstore can direct you to these titles or order them for you. If a book is out of print, check with a used bookstore or an antiquity dealer.

Devotional books

My Utmost for His Highest, Oswald Chambers
Morning and Evening, Charles Spurgeon
Streams in the Desert, Lettie B. Cowman

Books on prayer

Power Through Prayer, E. M. Bounds
Quiet Talks on Prayer, S. D. Gordon
A Diary of Private Prayer, John Baillie
31 Days of Praise, Ruth Myers